D1327321

COLLECTED PROSE

OF

JAMES ELROY FLECKER

AMS PRESS
NEW YORK

Collected Prose

James Elroy Flecker

London

G. Bell and Sons

Mcmxx

Library of Congress Cataloging in Publication Data

Flecker, James Elroy, 1884-1915.
    Collected prose.

    Reprint of the 1920 ed. published by G. Bell,
London
    CONTENTS: Tales and sketches.—The Grecians—
Critical Studies.
PR6011.L4A16   1976   828'.9'1208   75-41096
ISBN 0-404-14541-8

Reprinted from the edition of 1920, London
First AMS edition published in 1976
Manufactured in the United States of America

AMS PRESS INC.
NEW YORK, N.Y.

PREFATORY NOTE

IN 1916 Mr. Secker published Flecker's "Collected Poems." This volume contains all the Prose that he reprinted, or would probably have reprinted, except his novel "The King of Alsander." There remain to be published his Plays, of which "Hassan" is certainly the greatest thing he did. Of the pieces now reprinted "The Last Generation" was published as a booklet by the New Age Press, and certain others in the "New Statesman," the "Monthly Review," the "English Review," the "Cambridge Review," the "Nineteenth Century," the "Saturday Westminster Gazette," to the editors of all of which thanks are due. The first essay on John Davidson was written when he was an undergraduate; others, too, were very early.

CONTENTS

TALES AND SKETCHES

THE GRECIANS

CONTENTS

CRITICAL STUDIES

I

TALES AND SKETCHES

THE LAST GENERATION[1]

A STORY OF THE FUTURE

INTRODUCTION

I HAD been awake for I know not how many hours that summer dawn while the sun came over the hills and coloured the beautiful roses in my mother's garden. As I lay drowsily gazing through the window, I thought I had never known a morning so sultry, and yet so pleasant. Outside not a leaf stirred; yet the air was fresh, and the madrigal notes of the birds came to me with a peculiar intensity and clearness. I listened intently to the curious sound of trilling, which drew nearer and nearer, until it seemed to merge into a whirring noise that filled the room and crowded at my ears. At first I could see nothing, and lay in deadly fear of the unknown; but soon I thought I saw rims and sparks of spectral fire floating through the pane. Then I heard some one say: " I am the Wind." But the voice was so like that of an old friend whom one sees again after many years that my terror departed, and I asked simply why the Wind had come.

" I have come to you," he replied, " because you are

[1] Reprinted by kind permission of Messrs. Cecil Palmer and Hayward.

the first man I have discovered who is after my own heart. You whom others call dreamy and capricious, volatile and headstrong, you whom some accuse of weakness, others of unscrupulous abuse of power, you I know to be a true son of Æolus, a fit inhabitant for those caves of boisterous song."

"Are you the North Wind or the East Wind?" said I. "Or do you blow from the Atlantic? Yet if those be your feathers that shine upon the pane like yellow and purple threads, and if it be through your influence that the garden is so hot to-day, I should say you were the lazy South Wind, blowing from the countries that I love."

"I blow from no quarter of the Earth," replied the voice. "I am not in the compass. I am a little unknown Wind, and I cross not Space but Time. If you will come with me I will take you not over countries but over centuries, not directly, but waywardly, and you may travel where you will. You shall see Napoleon, Caesar, Pericles, if you command. You may be anywhere in the world at any period. I will show you some of my friends, the poets. . . ."

"And may I drink red wine with Praxiteles, or with Catullus beside his lake?"

"Certainly, if you know enough Latin and Greek, and can pronounce them intelligently."

"And may I live with Thais or Rhodope, or some wild Assyrian queen?"

"Unless they are otherwise employed, certainly."

"Ah, Wind of Time," I continued with a sigh, "we men of this age are rotten with book-lore, and with a yearning for the past. And wherever I asked to go among those ancient days, I should soon get dissatisfied, and weary your bright wings. I will be no pillar of salt, a sterile portent in a sterile desert. Carry me forward, Wind of Time. What is there going to be ?"

The Wind put his hand over my eyes.

I

AT BIRMINGHAM TOWN HALL

" This is our first stopping place," said a voice from the points of flame.

I opened my eyes expecting to see one of those extravagant scenes that imaginative novelists love to depict. I was prepared to find the upper air busy with aeroplanes and the earth beneath given over to un-bridled debauch. Instead, I discovered myself seated on a tall electric standard, watching a crowd assembled before what I took to be Birmingham Town Hall. I was disappointed in this so tame a sight, until it flashed across me that I had never seen an English crowd preserve such an orderly and quiet demeanour; and a more careful inspection assured me that although no man wore a uniform, every man carried a rifle. They were obviously waiting for some one to come and address them from the balcony of the Town Hall, which was festooned with red flags. As the curtains were pulled aside I caught a momentary glimpse of an old person whose face I shall never forget, but apparently it was not for him that the breathless crowd was waiting. The man who finally appeared on the balcony was an individual not more than thirty years old, with a black beard and green eyes. At the sound of acclamation which greeted him he burst

out into a loud laugh; then with a sudden seriousness he held up his hand and began to address his
followers:

"I have but few words for you, my army, a few
bitter words. Need I encourage men to fight who
have staked their existence to gain mastery? We
cannot draw back; never will the cries of the
slaughtered thousands we yearned to rescue from a
more protracted, more cruel misery than war, make
us forget the myriads who still await the supreme
mercy of our revenge.

"For centuries and for centuries we endured the
March of that Civilization which now, by the weapons
of her own making, we have set forth to destroy. We,
men of Birmingham, dwellers in this hideous town
unvisited by sun or moon, long endured to be told
that we were in the van of progress, leading Humanity
year by year along her glorious path. And, looking
around them, the wise men saw the progress of
civilization, and what was it? What did it mean?
Less country, fewer savages, deeper miseries, more
millionaires, and more museums. So to-day we march
on London.

"Let us commemorate, my friends, at this last hour,
a great, if all unwitting benefactor, the protomartyr of
our cause. You remember that lank follower of the
Newest Art, who lectured to us once within these
very walls? He it was who first expounded to us the
beauty of Birmingham, the artistic majesty of tall
chimneys, the sombre glory of furnaces, the deep
mystery of smoke, the sad picturesqueness of scrap-

heaps and of slag. Then we began to hate our lives
in earnest; then we arose and struck. Even now I
shudder when I think of that lecturer's fate, and
with a feeling of respect I commemorate his words
to-day.

"On, then! You need not doubt of my victory, nor
of my power. Some of you will die, but you know
that death is rest. You do not need to fear the sombre
fireworks of a mediaeval Hell, nor yet the dreary dis-
sipations of a Methodist Heaven. Come, friends, and
march on London!"

They heard him in deep silence; there was a gentle
stir of preparation; they faded far below me.

II

THE PROCLAMATION

AT a point ten years farther along that dusky road
the Wind set me down in a prodigious room. I had
never before seen so large and splendid a construction,
so gracefully embellished, so justly proportioned. The
shape was elliptical, and it seemed as if the architect
had drawn his inspiration from the Coliseum at Rome.
This Hall, however, was much larger, and had the
additional distinction of a roof, which, supported by a
granite column, was only rendered visible from beneath
by means of great bosses of clear gold. Galleries ran
round the walls, and there was even a corkscrew
balustrade winding up round the central pillar. Every
part of the building was crowded with people. There
seemed to be no window in the place, so that I could
not tell whether or no it was night. The whole
assembly was illuminated by a thousand electric discs,
and the ventilation was almost perfectly planned on a
system to me entirely strange. There was a raised
throne at one end of the building, on which sat a King
decently dressed in black. I recognized the green-
eyed man, and learnt that his name was Harris,
Joshua Harris. The entire body of the Hall was filled
by soldiers in mud-coloured tunics and waterproof
boots. These were the men that had conquered the
world.

As soon as the populace were well assembled the King made a sign to his Herald, who blew so sudden and terrific a blast with his trumpet that the multitude stopped their chattering with a start. The Herald proceeded to bawl a proclamation through his megaphone. I heard him distinctly, but should never have been able to reproduce his exact words, had not the Wind very kindly handed to me one of the printed copies for free distribution which it had wafted from a chair. The proclamation ran thus:

" *I, Joshua Harris, by right of conquest and in virtue of my intelligence, King of Britain, Emperor of the two Americas, and Lord High Suzerain of the World, to the Princes, Presidents, and Peoples of the said World,— Greeting. Ye know that in days past an old man now dead showed me how man's dolorous and fruitless sojourn on this globe might cease by his own act and wisdom; how pain and death and the black Power that made us might be frustrated of their accustomed prey. Then I swore an oath to fulfil that old man's scheme, and I gathered my followers, who were the miserable men, and the hungry men, and we have conquered all there is to conquer by our cannon and by our skill. Already last year I gave public notice, in the proclamation of Vienna, in the proclamation of Cairo, in the proclamation of Pekin, and in the proclamation of Rio Janeiro, that all bearing of children must cease, and that all women should be permanently sterilized according to the prescription of Doctor Smith. Therefore to-day, since there is no remote African plain, no island far away in the deep South Seas where our forces are not supreme and our agents not vigilant, I make my final proclamation to you, my army, and to you, Princes, Presidents, and Peoples of this World, that from this hour forth there be no child born of any woman, or, if born, that it be slain with its father and its mother* (a fainting woman had here to be carried out), *and to you, my terrestrial forces, I entrust the execution of my commands.*

"*Joy then be with you, my people, for the granaries are full of corn and wine that I have laid up, sufficient for many years to come; joy be with you, since you are the last and noblest generation of mankind, and since Doctor Smith by his invention, and I by my wise pre-vision, have enabled you to live not only without payment and without work* (loud cheers from the galleries), *but also with luxury and splendour, and with all the delights, and none of the dangers, of universal love.*"

I expected this proclamation to be followed by an outburst of applause; but instead, the whole multitude sat calm and motionless. Looking round I was struck by the hideous appearance of mankind. It was especially revolting to look at the ears of the soldiers in front, who had their backs turned to me. These stuck out from the bullet-like heads, and made the men look like two-handled teapots on stands. Yet here and there appeared in the galleries some woman's countenance beautified by the sorrows of our race, or some tall youth whose eyes expressed the darkest de-termination. The silence seemed to gather in folds. I was studying drowsily the Asiatic dresses and the nude people from Melanesia, when I heard a noise which I thought was that of the Wind. But I saw it was the King, who had begun to laugh. It was a very strange noise indeed, and very strange laughter.

III

THE MUTUAL EXTERMINATION CLUB

"YOU would perhaps like to stay here some time," said the Wind, "and look around. You will then understand the significance of this generation more clearly, and you may observe some interesting incidents."

I was standing with one or two other people outside a pseudo-Chinese erection, which I at first took to be a cricket pavilion, and then saw to be the headquarters of a rifle club. I apprehended from the placards that I was in Germany, and inquired in the language of the country, which I understand very well, what was the object of this rifle practice, and whether there was any thought of war.

The man to whom I addressed myself, an adipose person with iron-rimmed spectacles and a kindly, intelligent face, seemed surprised at my question.

"You must be a stranger," he said. "This is our very notable *Vertildungsverein.*"

I understood: it was a Club for Mutual Extermination.

I then noticed that there were no ordinary targets, and that the cadets were pointing their rifles at a bearded man who stood with a covered pipe in his mouth, leaning against a tree some two hundred yards away.

After the report the bearded man held up both hands.

"That is to signify that he has been completely missed," said the fat gentleman. "One hand, wounded; two hands, missed. And that is reasonable (*vernunftig*), because if he were dead he could not raise either."

I approved the admirable logic of the rule, and supposed that the man would now be allowed to go free.

"Oh, yes, according to the rules," he answered, "he certainly is allowed to go free; but I do not think his sense of honour would permit him so to do."

"Is he then of very noble family?" I inquired.

"Not at all; he is a scientist. We have a great many scientists in our club. They are all so disappointed at the way in which human progress has been impeded, and at the impossibility of a continuous evolution of knowledge-accumulation, that they find no more attraction in life. And he is dead this time," he continued, shading his eyes to look, as soon as a second report had flashed.

"By the way," I asked, "I suppose you only exterminate—er—members of the club?"

The fellow smiled with a little disdain. "Oh, it would be illegal for us to exterminate outsiders. But of course if you would like to join. . . ."

"Why, that's never a woman going over to the tree!" I cried.

"Oh yes, we have quite a number of intellectual women and upper-class ladies of advanced ideas in the club. But I do not think that lady is an intellectual she is more probably a passion-wreck."

She was indeed a very handsome woman in the prime of life, dressed with a little too much ostentation and coquetry in a sleeveless, transparent white blouse and a skirt to match.

My informant turned round to a skinny young student with hog's-bristle hair, and made some vulgar jest about its "being a pity to waste such a good piece of flesh." He was a super-man, and imagined, falsely I believe, that an air of bluff cynicism, a Teutonic attempt at heartiness, was the true outward sign of inward superiority. The young man fired, and the woman raised the arm that was not shattered by the bullet. He fired again, and she fell on her knees, this time with a scream.

" I think you had better have a shot," said the sharp-shooter to my man. " I'm rather bad at this."

Indeed his hand was shaking violently.

My interlocutor bowed, and went over to take the rifle. The skinny student took his place by my side, and began talking to me as well. " He 's an infallible shot that Müller there," he said, nodding at my former companion. . . . "Didn't I tell you?"

To my great relief the passion-wrecked lady fell dead. I was getting wildly excited, rent between horror and curiosity.

" You see that man in the plumed hat?" said the student. " He is coming round to say on whom the lot has fallen. Ah, he is coming this way, and making a sign at me. Good-day, sir," he said, taking off his hat with a deep and jerky bow. " I am afraid we must continue our conversation another time."

IV

THE EPISODE OF THE BABY

As soon as I turned away, rather horrified, from the merry proceedings of the Mutual Extermination Club, I seemed to be in England, or perhaps in America. At all events I was walking along a dusty highway in the midst of an inquisitive crowd. In front of me half-a-dozen members of the International Police Force (their tunics and boots gave me to understand their quality) were dragging along a woman who held a baby in her arms. A horror-struck and interested multitude surged behind, and rested only when the woman was taken into a large and disgusting edifice with iron gates. Aided by my distinguished appearance and carriage, I succeeded after some difficulty in persuading the Chief Gaoler to let me visit the cell where the mother was lodged, previous to undergoing an execution which would doubtless be as unpleasant as prolonged. I found a robust, apple-cheeked woman, very clean and neat, despite her forlorn condition and the rough handling the guards had used to her. She confessed to me with tears that she had been in her day a provincial courtesan, and that she had been overcome by desire to have a child, " just to see what it was like." She had therefore employed all imaginable shifts to avoid being injected with Smithia, and had fled with an old admirer to a lonely cave, where she had brought forth her child. " And a pretty boy too," she added, wringing her hands, " and only fourteen months old."

She was so heart-broken that I did not like to ask her any more questions till she had recovered, for fear her anwers should be unintelligible. Finally, as I desired to learn matters that were of common knowledge to the rest of the world, and was not anxious to arouse suspicion, I represented myself as a cultured foreigner who had just been released from a *manicomio*, and was therefore naturally in a state of profound ignorance on all that appertained to Modern History. I felt indeed that I would never have a better chance of gathering information than from conversation with this solitary woman. It would be her pleasure, not her duty, to instruct me.

So I began by asking how the diminishing numbers of the military could keep a sufficient watch, and how it was that every one submitted so meekly to the proclamation. She answered that the police recruited themselves yearly from the more active and noble-minded of the people, that custom had a lot to do with the submissive attitude of mankind, and that apart from that, there was a great resolve abroad to carry out the project of King Harris to fulfilment. She went on to inform me that Smithia was tasteless, and would act even when drunk at meals, and not merely as an injection, that it acted on both sexes, and that it was otherwise innocuous. By now most of the well-springs, reservoirs, and cisterns had been contaminated by the fluid, of which large quantities had been prepared at a very cheap price. After gleaning sundry other details, I thanked her heartily and left the cell.

Outside in the courtyard I discovered a large concourse of people examining the baby, who was naturally enough an object of extreme wonder to the whole country-side. The women called it a duck, and used other pet names that were not then in fashion, but most of the men thought it was an ugly little brat at best. The child was seated on a cushion, and despite his mother's absence was crowing vigorously and kicking with puny force. There was some debate as to how it should be killed. Some were for boiling and eating it; others were for hitting it on the head with a club. However, the official who held the cushion brought the conference to a close by inadvertently dropping the child on to the flags, and thereby breaking its neck.

V

THE FLORENTINE LEAGUE

I FEEL certain on reflection that the scene of the last episode must have been America, for I remember returning to Europe on a French boat which landed me at Havre, and immediately taking the train to Paris. As I passed through Normandy, I saw hardly a soul stirring in the villages, and the small houses were all in a most dilapidated condition. There was no more need for farms, and villagers in their loneliness were flocking to the towns. Even the outer suburbs of Paris were mere masses of flaked and decaying plaster. An unpleasant crash into the buffers of Saint Lazare reminded me that the engine was being driven by an amateur; indeed, we had met the Dieppe train at Rouen, sent a pilot engine ahead to clear the way, and then raced it to Paris on the up-line amid enthusiastic cheers. We won, but were badly shaken.

We left the train beside the platform, trusting to the Church Missionary Society man to put it away in the engine-shed. These excellent philanthropists were unwearying in their efforts to prevent needless oss of life, and such work as was still done in the world was performed almost entirely by them and by members of kindred British Protestant societies. They wore a blue badge to distinguish themselves,

and were ordered about by every one. At the call of
" Anglais, Anglais! " some side-whiskered man would
immediately run up to obey the summons, and you
could send him to get food from the Store for you,
and he would be only too pleased. They would also
cook hot dinners.

I walked through the Boulevard Montmartre, and
at every step I took I became more profoundly miserable. One had called Paris the pleasant city, the
fairest city in the world, in the days before the
Proclamation; for one found it vibrating with beauty
and life. And now assuredly it was supremely a city
of pleasure, for there was no work to be done at all.
So no artist ever took any trouble now, since there
was neither payment nor fame attainable; and wonderful caricatures of philanthropists scribbled on the pavement or elsewhere, or clever ribald songs shrieking
out of gramophones were the only reminder of that
past and beautiful Paris that I had known. There
was a fatuous and brutal expression on most of the
faces, and the people seemed to be too lazy to do
anything except drink and fondle. Even the lunatics
attracted but little attention. There was a flying-
machine man who was determined, as he expressed
it, " that it should not be said of the human race that
it never flew." Even the " Anglais " were tired of
helping him with his machine, which he was quietly
building on the Place de l'Opéra—a mass of intricate
wires, bamboos, and paper boxes; and the inventor
himself frequently got lost as he climbed cheerily
among the rigging.

Weary of all this, I slept, alone, in one of the public beds, and early next morning I clambered up the sacred slope of the Butte to see the sunrise. The great silence of early morning was over the town, a deathly and unnatural stillness. As I stood leaning over the parapet, thinking miserably, a young man came up the hill slowly yet gracefully, so that it was a pleasure to look at him. His face was sad and noble, and as I had never thought to see nobility again, I hoped he would be a friend to me. However, he turned himself almost roughly, and said:

"Why have you come here?"

"To look at the fallen city I loved long ago," I replied, with careless sorrow.

"Have you then also read of the old times in books?" he said, looking round at me with large bright eyes.

"Yes, I have read many books," said I, trying to evade the subject. "But will you forgive me if I ask an impertinent question?"

"Nothing coming from you, sir, could be impertinent."

"I wanted to ask how old you are, because you seem so young. You seem to be only seventeen."

"You could tell me nothing more delightful," the young man replied, with a gentle, yet strong and deep intonation. "I am indeed one of the youngest men alive—I am twenty-two years old. And I am looking for the last time on the city of Paris."

"Do not say that," I cried. "All this may be horrible, but it cannot be as dull as Death. Surely there

must be some place in the world where we could live
among beauty; some other folk besides ourselves who
are still poets. Why should one die until life becomes
hopelessly ugly and deformed?"

"I am not going to kill myself, as you seem to
think," said the young man. "I am going, and I pray
and implore you to come with me, to a place after
your heart and mine, that some friends have prepared. It is a garden, and we are a League. I have
already been there three months, and I have put on
these horrible clothes for one day only, in obedience
to a rule of our League, that every one should go out
once a year to look at the world around. We are
thinking of abolishing the rule."

"How pleasant and beautiful it sounds!"

"It is, and will you come with me there right
now?"

"Shall I be admitted?"

"My word will admit you at once. Come this way
with me. I have a motor at the bottom of the hill."

During the journey I gathered much information
about the League, which was called the Florentine
League. It had been formed out of the youngest
"years" of the race, and its members had been chosen
for their taste and elegance. For although few parents
of the day had thought it worth while to teach their
children anything more recondite than their letters
and tables, yet some of the boys and girls had devel-
oped a great desire for knowledge, and an exceeding
great delight in Poetry, Art, Music, and all beautiful
sights and sounds.

" We live," he said, " apart from the world, like that merry company of gentlefolk who, when the plague was raging at Florence, left the city, and retiring to a villa in the hills, told each other those enchanting tales. We enjoy all that Life, Nature, and Art can give us, and Love has not deserted the garden, but still draws his golden bow. It is no crippled and faded Eros of the City that dwells among us, but the golden-thighed God himself. For we do all things with refinement, and not like those outside, seeing to it that in all our acts we keep our souls and bodies both delicate and pure."

We came to the door of a long wall, and knocked. White-robed attendants appeared in answer to our summons, and I was stripped, bathed, and anointed by their deft hands. All the while a sound of singing and subdued laughter made me eager to be in the garden. I was then clothed in a very simple white silk garment with a gold clasp; the open door let sunshine in upon the tiles, and my friend, also clothed in silk, awaited me. We walked out into the garden, which was especially noticeable for those flowers which have always been called old-fashioned — I mean hollyhocks, sweet-william, snap-dragons, and Canterbury bells, which were laid out in regular beds. Everywhere young men and women were together: some were walking about idly in the shade; some played at fives; some were reading to each other in the arbours. I was shown a Grecian temple in which was a library, and dwelling-places near it. I afterwards asked a girl called Fiore di Fiamma what books the Florentines preferred to read, and she told me that they loved the Poets best, not so much the serious and strenuous as those whose vague and fleeting fancies wrap the soul in an enchanting sorrow.

I asked : "Do you write songs, Fiore di Fiamma?"

"Yes, I have written a few, and music for them."

"Do sing me one, and I will play the guitar."

So she sang me one of the most mournful songs I had ever heard, a song which had given up all hope of fame, written for the moment's laughter or for the moment's tears.

"Wind," I said that night, "stay with me many years in the garden."

But it was not the Wind I kissed.

VI

OUTSIDE

I PASSED many years in that sad, enchanted place, dreaming at times of my mother's roses, and of friends that I had known before, and watching our company grow older and fewer. There was a rule that no one should stay there after their thirty-seventh birthday, and some old comrades passed weeping from us to join the World Outside. But most of them chose to take poison and to die quietly in the Garden; we used to burn their bodies, singing, and set out their urns on the grass. In time I became Prince of the Garden: no one knew my age, and I grew no older; yet my Flame-Flower knew when I intended to die. Thus we lived on undisturbed, save for some horrible shout that rose from time to time from beyond the walls; but we were not afraid, as we had cannon mounted at our gates. At last there were twelve of us left in the precinct of delight, and we decided to die all together on the eve of the Queen's birthday. So we made a great feast and held good cheer, and had the poison prepared and cast lots. The first lot fell to Fiore di Fiamma, and the last lot to me; whereat all applauded. I watched my Queen, who had never seemed to me as noble as then, in her mature and majestic beauty. She kissed me, and drank, and the others drank, became very pale, and fell to earth. Then I, rising with a last paean of exultation, raised the cup to my lips.

But that moment the trees and flowers bent beneath a furious storm, and the cup was wrenched out of my hand by a terrific blast and sent hurtling to the ground. I saw the rainbow-coloured feathers flashing, and for a second I saw the face of the Wind himself. I trembled, and, sinking into my chair, buried my face in my hands. A wave of despair and loneliness broke over me. I felt like a drowning man.

"Take me back, Lord of the Wind!" I cried. "What am I doing among these dead aesthetes? Take me back to the country where I was born, to the house where I am at home, to the things I used to handle, to the friends with whom I talked, before man went mad. I am sick of this generation that cannot strive or fight, these people of one idea, this doleful, ageing world. Take me away!"

But the Wind replied in angry tones, not gently as of old :

"Is it thus you treat me, you whom I singled out from men? You have forgotten me for fifteen years; you have wandered up and down a garden, oblivious of all things that I had taught you, incurious, idle, listless, effeminate. Now I have saved you from dying a mock death, like a jester in a tragedy ; and in time I will take you back, for that I promised ; but first you shall be punished as ,you deserve." So saying, the Wind raised me aloft and set me beyond the wall.

I dare not describe—I fear to remember the un-
utterable loathing of the three years I spent outside.
The unhappy remnant of a middle-aged mankind
was gradually exchanging lust for gluttony. Crowds
squatted by day and by night round the Houses of
Dainty Foods that had been stocked by Harris the
King; there was no youthful face to be found among
them, and scarcely one that was not repulsively deformed with the signs of lust, cunning, and debauch.
At evening there were incessant fires of crumbling
buildings, and fat women made horrible attempts at
revelry. There seemed to be no power of thought in
these creatures. The civilization of ages had fallen
from them like a worthless rag from off their backs.
Europeans were as bestial as Hottentots, and the
noblest thing they ever did was to fight; for sometimes a fierce desire of battle seized them, and then
they tore each other passionately with teeth and nails.

I cannot understand it even now. Surely there
should have been some Puritans somewhere, or some
Philosophers waiting to die with dignity and honour.
Was it that there was no work to do? Or that there
were no children to love? Or that there was nothing
young in the World? Or that all beautiful souls
perished in the garden?

I think it must have been the terrible thought of
approaching extinction that obsessed these distracted
men. And perhaps they were not totally depraved.
There was a rough fellowship among them, a desire
to herd together; and for all that they fought so
much, they fought in groups. They never troubled

to look after the sick and the wounded, but what could they do?

One day I began to feel that I too was one of them —I, who had held aloof in secret ways so long, joined the gruesome company in their nightly dance, and sat down to eat and drink their interminable meal. Suddenly a huge, wild, naked man appeared in front of the firelight, a prophet, as it appeared, who prophesied not death but life. He flung out his lean arms and shouted at us: "In vain have you schemed and lingered and died, O Last Generation of the Damned. For the cities shall be built again, and the mills shall grind anew, and the church bells shall ring, and the Earth be re-peopled with new miseries in God's own time."

I could not bear to hear this fellow speak. Here was one of the old sort of men, the men that talked evil, and murmured about God. "Friends," I said, turning to the Feasters, "we will have no skeletons like that at our feast." So saying I seized a piece of flaming wood from the fire, and rushed at the man. He struggled fiercely, but he had no weapon, and I beat him about the head till he fell, and death rattled in his throat—rattled with what seemed to me a most familiar sound. I stood aghast; then wiped the blood from the man's eyes and looked into them.

"Who are you?" I exclaimed. "I have seen you before; I seem to know the sound of your voice and the colour of your eyes. Can you speak a word and tell us your story, most unhappy prophet, before you die?"

"Men of the Last Generation," said the dying man, raising himself on his elbow—"Men of the Last Generation, I am Joshua Harris, your King."

As brainless frogs who have no thought or sense in them, yet shrink when they are touched, and swim when the accustomed water laves their eager limbs, so did these poor creatures feel a nerve stirring within them, and unconsciously obey the voice which had commanded them of old. As though the mere sound of his tremulous words conveyed an irresistible mandate, the whole group came shuffling nearer. All the while they preserved a silence that made me afraid, so reminiscent was it of that deadly hush that had followed the Proclamation, of the quiet army starting for London, and especially of that mysterious and sultry morning so many years ago when the roses hung their enamelled heads and the leaves were as still as leaves of tin or copper. They sat down in circles round the fire, maintaining an orderly disposition, like a stray battalion of some defeated army which is weary of fruitless journeys in foreign lands, but still remembers discipline and answers to command. Meanwhile, the dying man was gathering with a noiseless yet visible effort every shred of strength from his massive limbs, and preparing to give them his last message. As he looked round on that frightful crowd great tears, that his own pain and impending doom could never have drawn from him, filled his strange eyes.

"Forgive me—forgive me," he said at last, clearly enough for all to hear. "If any of you still know what mercy is, or the meaning of forgiveness, say a kind word to me. Loving you, relying on humanity and myself, despising the march of Time and the power of Heaven, I became a false redeemer, and took upon my back the burden of all sin. But how was I to know, my people, I who am only a man, whither my plans for your redemption would lead? Have none of you a word to say?

"Is there no one here who remembers our fighting days? Where are the great lieutenants who stood at my side and cheered me with counsel? Where are Robertson, Baldwin, and Andrew Spencer? Are there none of the old set left?"

He brushed the tears and blood from his eyes and gazed into the crowd. Pointing joyously to an old man who sat not far away he called out: "I know you, Andrew, from that great scar on your forehead. Come here, Andrew, and that quickly."

The old man seemed neither to hear nor understand him, but sat like all the rest, blinking and unresponsive.

"Andrew," he cried, "you must know me! Think of Brum and South Melton Street. Be an Englishman, Andrew—come and shake hands!"

The man looked at him with staring, timid eyes; then shuddered all over, scrambled up from the ground, and ran away.

"It does not matter," murmured the King of the World. "There are no men left. I have lived in the desert, and I saw there that which I would I had seen long ago—visions that came too late to warn me. For a time my Plan has conquered; but that greater Plan shall be victorious in the end."

I was trying to staunch the wounds I had inflicted, and I hoped to comfort him, but he thrust me aside.

" I know that no man of this generation could have killed me. I have nothing in common with you, bright Spirit. It was not you I loved, not for you I fought and struggled, but for these. I do not want to be reminded, by that light of reason shining in your eyes, of what we were all of us, once. It was a heroic age, when good and evil lived together, and misery bound man to man. Yet I will not regret what I have done. I ask forgiveness not of God, but of Man; and I claim the gratitude of thousands who are unknown, and unknown shall ever remain. For ages and ages God must reign over an empty kingdom, since I have brought to an end one great cycle of centuries. Tell me, Stranger, was I not great in my day? "

He fell back, and the Wind that took his Spirit carried me also into space.

VII

THE LAST MAN

THE Wind bore me onwards more than forty years, and I found seated beside a granary half-a-dozen wrinkled and very aged men, whose faces were set with a determination to go on living to the bitter end. They were delirious, and naked; they tore their white beards; they mumbled and could not speak. The great beasts came out of the forest by night softly and gazed at them with their lantern eyes, but never did them harm. All day long they ate and slept or wandered a little aimlessly about. During that year four of them died.

Afterwards I saw the last two men. One of them was lying on the ground gasping passionately for breath, his withered limbs awry with pain. I could see that he had been a magnificent man in his youth. As his old friend died, the Last of the Race remembered his Humanity. He bent down, kissed the livid lips, carefully and tearfully closed the filmed red eyes. He even tried to scratch a grave with his long finger-nails, but soon despaired. He then went away, plodding as fast as he could hobble, weeping silently, afraid of the Dead. In the afternoon he came to a vast city, where many corpses lay; and about nightfall, when the stars were shining, he came to a massive half-ruined Dome that had been used for the worship of some God. Entering, he tottered towards the altar, which still stood, half-buried in stone-dust and flakes; and reaching up to a great bronze Crucifix that stood upon it, with his dying strength he clasped to his arms the Emblem of our Sorrow.

.   .   .   .   .

I saw the vast Halls and Palaces of men falling in slowly, decaying, crumbling, destroyed by nothing but the rains and the touch of Time.   And looking again I saw wandering over and above the ruins, moving curiously about, myriads of brown, hairy, repulsive little apes.

One of them was building a fire with sticks.

N' JAWK

THE shade of Archdeacon Puxley, rationalist, idealist, and divine, was disconcerted at its own existence. As a cleric that Archdeacon had, of course, strictly upheld the doctrine of Immortality as expounded in the Apocalypse. Secretly, we regret to state, Puxley had held different views. This was probably the fault of that pernicious system of education which disturbs the simple faith of our young men with a course of purely Pagan philosophy. At all events, there can be no doubt that Peter Puxley, undergraduate, after three years' residence in the University of Oxford, believed neither in Inspiration nor in Immortality, nor even in that sweet Idealism which reconciled the philosopher Hegel to the Lutheran Church. Puxley's beliefs might have affected Puxley's conduct, for he had a logical, even a practical, mind; but his character was steady and firm; nor could the insidious worm of Infidelity eat away that goodly treasure of sound morals which he had inherited from a long line of ancestors, all Christians, and some in Orders. " There is no reason now," Puxley had said to himself, as he paced his tastefully furnished rooms on the day on which he felt himself forced to abandon even Hegel—" no reason, I say, why I should not behave like an absolute beast. But I should not enjoy it: that is what is so unfortunate. It is true that I eat rather a lot; but I have no longing whatever to commit arson, rape, murder, or anything else that might entail unpleasant consequences. I desire a life of studious ease; and where shall I obtain my desire save in the bosom of the Anglican Church? Infidelity is always put down to youth and conceit in this age; whereas the priest is honoured and respected. Of course," he continued, looking at his mirror, " I shall be a high churchman, very high. It is a much better thing socially; besides, I have the High Church face."

So Peter Puxley, undergraduate, determined to realize himself in all tranquillity, and in due course he became the Rev. P. Puxley, and a fellow of his College. His sermons on the relation between Platonic and Christian Love soon attracted attention, and he was admitted into the fraternity of gaiters. But those whom the gods love die young; and Puxley was still what might be called a middle-aged man when a violent colic took him from us and blasted that promising career. But that complete annihilation of the Ego, which his infidelity expected and his hypocrisy deserved, did not overtake him after death. He became, to his alarm, a vulgar, anthropomorphic ghost, in fact, a gaseous vertebrate, to use the eloquent term of the admirable Haeckel. But there was worse than this. The soul of our learned friend was being propelled through infinity in a most extraordinary fashion. Mysteriously yet irresistibly impelled, his astral body proceeded in a continuous succession of violent jerks, and every seventh jerk produced a complete somersault.

It was after completing some hundreds of these gyrations, that he discovered himself entangled in the soul of Slimber. Slimber was a poet. He had published an exquisite volume of verse in the Doreskin Library of modern Masterpieces. The volume, not fifty pages long, but fine in quality, was printed on one side of the page, and was dedicated to a Lady. Intimacies of this sort, mentally so exhausting, had combined with a too sensitive taste in liqueurs to carry him off at an early age. His articles to "Tit Bits" and "Pearson's Weekly," though the real source of his modest revenue, were even less well known than his poems. Yet his unsigned essay on "How to make money by writing" was not only deservedly popular among that wide public to which "Tit Bits" appeals, but had also saved him from death by starvation.

At present this fanciful and slender shade was simply clad in an undervest. For though we carry nothing into this world, yet it is not so sure that we can carry nothing out: for not only do our good deeds remain after us, but our nightshirts as well, or whatever apparel we may wear at the supreme moment of our Destiny. Hence do so many ghosts wear draperies of white linen; hence the appearance of Slimber in his undervest; and hence, too, the pyjamas and white woollen bedsocks which adorned the robuster wraith of Archdeacon Puxley.

This ecclesiastical spectre, at great peril to his individuality, extricated himself from the soul of Slimber, and as they went travelling on together in parallel paths remarked to his new-found companion: "This is absurd."

"Isn't it?" said Slimber. "Delightfully so."

"I see nothing delightful in it at all," said Puxley. "It is perfectly irrational and extremely undignified."

"Wash," said Slimber rudely, "what could be more charming than this our progress among the speckled stars, varied as it is by the performance of this exquisitely irrelevant turn." And he gracefully convoluted.

"Is this the way we are to realize ourselves?" wailed the philosopher-priest, taking refuge in his long abandoned Idealism. "I was not made for this." And he in his turn convoluted.

"Insensate Philistine," began Slimber; but at this moment their course was abruptly arrested, and they found themselves hanging head downwards in an Oriental Palace. In front of them, sitting the right way up, was a sort of god. It had one large eye in the middle of its forehead, and an amorphous belly. It was unclothed, and coloured pink and green. It or he was surrounded by guards in uniform and by several naked yet attractive savage ladies of a Burmese type and colour.

"Turn the fat 'un round," said the God, laconically, but in perfect English, to his guards. "Turn him round, I say. He wobbles so he makes me dizzy."

The guards seized Puxley and planted him on the ground, leaving poor Slimber still inverted.

"Now then," said the God to Puxley. "What have you to say for yourself? What have you ever done to honour me?"

"Sir," said Puxley, "I do not even know your name."

"My name is N' Jawk," said the God, booming. "What have you ever done for me? Have you garrotted any women in my honour? Have you nicked your ears in my service? Have you even sacrificed one poor little pig in my honour? Why, you don't even know my name!"

"Sir," said Puxley, "I am confused. I cannot think. If you could show me to an apartment where I could realize myself in private. . . ."

"Realize yourself, indeed!" said N' Jawk. "You will probably be made into porridge. Answer my questions."

"But damn it," said Puxley, terrified. "This is perfectly unreasonable. I have always been a most moral man."

"Do you imagine that the little bit of reason I gave you to play with has anything to do with the truth?" snorted the Deity. "You bore me. Porridge!"

And the guards hustled Puxley away.

"Well, you wreck of a man," said the God, opening his mouth quite round, and turning to Slimber, who still hung by his feet, "what have you got to say?"

"Sir," said the Poet, with an attempt at an inverted bow, "I think I could talk better the ordinary way up."

"Sorry. I forgot," said N' Jawk. "Turn him round there. Now then!"

The Poet, now on his feet, took a step towards the throne and prostrated himself before N' Jawk.

"Lord of majesty and might," he began: "Most interesting and shining twi-colour Deity, beyond all expectation, delicate and rare, hear me, I pray, and attend to my supplication. I have worshipped you, O fantastic Spirit, all my days; and if I have not gar- rotted any women in your honour, I have well nigh strangled them many a time. I have lived as I liked, and followed no strange gods. O, most admirable of grotesques, most fascinating of paradoxes, turn me not into porridge. Let me stay here with these enchanting girls."

Whereupon one of the fairest of the young ladies took Slimber's hand and said to the God: "Yes, do let him stay and play with us, Papa; he looks so nice."

"All right," said N' Jawk, benevolently. "All right, my dears; he shall stay. But I'm hungry. Bring in that porridge."

PENTHEUS

ARE there any who do not know Pentheus, that harsh and surly tyrant who laid rude hands upon a God? Well might he wonder who was this long-haired, bright-cheeked stranger with the charms of Aphrodite in his eyes, who was disturbing the peace of his kingdom, and leading the girls into profitless and presumably immoral dances on the dappled hills. What would happen to the looms and the Theban cloth industry the while?

The stranger was the God Dionysus the terrible, he whom once unwitting Aegean pirates treacherously seized, and they would have borne him a slave of price to some odorous and languid city of the South; but he knew their thoughts, and became a Lion, and turned their oars to serpents, so that they leapt into the sea, dolphins and not men, and swim desolately on to this day. And he was the God Dionysus the merciful, who once himself had died, as Osiris, as Attis died, to benefit mankind. Born again, he gave them wine, without which, as the messenger says in the Bacchae, "there is no love nor any other pleasant thing left on earth." But how should Pentheus know this? He was a man who hated all nonsense, and was not given to dancing or to drink. A religious man, no doubt, he was one of those who believe in the moral and social benefits that religion confers, and was not over-interested in miracles and myths. It is hard to persuade a man of sense that you are an angel. The voice of Bromios, the earthquake and the fire that bring his house about his ears, the queer escape of the stranger from his prison in the stall, pain, but do not mystify his practical mind. The fire from Heaven is an unfortunate accident, extinguishable by buckets ; the stranger always was a clever, cunning fellow.

But when Pentheus hears that his own mother has joined the revellers, that the Maenads have driven the peasants before them, and are nearing the very gates of Thebes, he falls into a panic, honest fellow that he is ; without a moment's hesitation, like one of our intrepid Governors beyond the seas, he appeals to the military, and summons his armed police.

It is then that a most curious thing happens. The stranger turns his deep love-eyes on Pentheus, with no loving intent, and transforms him. He begins to long for a sight of those doings on Kithairon, if only to spy them out and to make better dispositions for his raid. In this spirit Mr. Stead goes to the theatre, or a Methodist to Monte Carlo.

Dazzled by the clear glance of the god, Pentheus begins to make himself ridiculous. The tempting, treacherous stranger decks him out as a woman and leads him through the city, the mock of his people. As he draws near Kithairon, he too feels the ecstasy; but he is always Pentheus. His madness is but a drunken parody of mystical exaltation. He dances

clumsily, he sees two suns, two city gates, and the god
like a bull before him. He cries out that his faith
can remove literal mountains, he loosens his belt,
and his gown goes all awry. The cruel god laughs
and ties it up for him. "It is a little wrong by the
right foot," says Pentheus, with superb fatuity; "but
the other side is perfectly correct." Then suddenly
the ludicrous man becomes puffed up with pride at
his daring. He will be quite wicked, and see what
those naughty girls are doing, dancing in the
night.

Disaster fell swiftly on his head. When they came
to the place appointed Dionysus bent down a pine-
tree and sat the poor fool on its trunk; he is shot up
into the air, and on that wild eminence of branches
becomes conspicuous to all. A voice calls the women,
who, led by Agave, his own mother, rush forward and
root up the tree with their white arms. Pentheus
falls. Death alone makes him tragic. Then he flung
off his head-dress, so that Agave should recognize
him and not kill him. Touching her cheek, he said:
"I am your son Pentheus, mother, whom you bore in
Echion's house; pity me, mother, and do not kill
your son for his sins." They foamed at the mouth
and tore him limb from limb. So he died, suffered
such a death as, according to dim legends, Dionysus
himself suffered of old.

This is the account of Euripides; but we cannot
believe that here was an end of Pentheus. Mr. Fraser
would doubtless say that he was a corn-spirit, a king
who died for his people and was hung upon a tree;

and that the fragments of his lacerated corpse were carried round the fields to fertilize them. If so, Pentheus should be sacrificed anew every Autumn and come to life every Spring. But whether this be true or not, I have discovered that Pentheus is immortal, that he has manifested himself many times since those legendary days of Thebes, and moreover, that he is alive to-day.

Many years after, in a land south-east of Hellas, there arose a successor to Dionysus, a preacher of joy. He advised men to cease fasting, to neglect the law and to honour above all things, love. He proclaimed a golden age of happiness and peace.

Pentheus, who was ruling at the time, could not stand this. All his philosophic idealism, all his respect for law and custom, was outraged by what appeared to him a wanton and anarchical subversion of principles that had stood the test of time. He had his revenge for his old maltreatment. Not he but the God was called the man of sorrows, not Pentheus hung upon the tree.

" Now," thought he, " I shall have no more of those deep love-eyes."

But the God rose again, a hundredfold stronger. His servants went forth to mountains and caves, saw visions and sang hymns, rejoicing in the mysteries of their salvation. Cold and heat, stripes and fasting, hurt them no more than they hurt the Maenads on the mountain.

Then Pentheus, seeing himself badly worsted, made friends with the God, as he had made friends with

Dionysus. He stipulated that the dancing should be more private, and that the Maenads and Satyrs should be less eccentrically clothed. He relegated the mystic feasts to the seventh day, and saw that all initiants were taught their duty to Pentheus. The rest of the week he kept them at the bitter loom.

He thus succeeded (for he was a very powerful king), in turning the religion into a support of his own power; and the worshippers began to neglect their deity. There was little joy to be found in his service now that there were no more dances or visions, nothing but an outward correctitude and inward impurity—for Pentheus was ever of the tribe of Angelo.

A little more than a hundred years ago a new God began to disturb the empire of Pentheus, a God of liberty and war, perhaps a new emanation of Mithras the Liberator, who also wore the red Phrygian cap. Pentheus pleaded for his life, for he found the ways of this new disturber short and sharp. " I am a brave man myself," he said ; " I am not at all averse to war; indeed, it is one of my favourite occupations ; and as for liberty, why, a reasonable freedom on a sound legal and moral basis has been my ideal for years."

The God with the Phrygian cap, however, merely laughed, seven times perhaps, as old magic liturgics say he laughed when the world was made; his servants rent Pentheus into more parts than he ever knew he possessed, and his blood streamed through all Europe.

But years had increased his power of resurrection:

no one will ever destroy Pentheus now. For he finds a Northern climate highly beneficial to his health, and thrives better on potatoes and beef than on olives and honey.

To-day a new God calls to him, a God who can find few to come to him from the vast kingdom of Pentheus. He does not taunt the tyrant; he tries to woo him instead. "Come out and love, Pentheus," he says softly; "leave your ridiculous concerns, your childish politics, your amusingly ugly towns. There are lands where sunlight and harmony are not yet dead; there are the absurdest poets leading lobsters on strings and charming all sylvan beasts by their pleasant ways. The girls are still dancing out in the fields; we have even found someone who still knows how to make a garland. Pentheus, come out and live!"

Then that man answers: "My dear sir, I am entirely with you. You must not imagine that in the midst of my more serious occupations I have neglected or even desired to neglect the Interests of Art. So impetuous you young divinities are, you know," he continues, with a smile, for he has lost his old surliness and become quite an affable and portly old fellow now. "I need only refer to my art galleries, to the royal academies, and to the great efforts I have made to provide all who come to the County Council schools with a sound grounding in English literature, starting with Beowulf, and tracing the gradual development of Idealism down to the death of Tennyson."

"Then you might take some interest, Pentheus, in those who are writing at the present day. Most of them have to add up figures or something equally absurd; and the rest are almost starving."

"Now come, come, there's the Civil Service pension. You can't expect me to look on these young men with favour. They don't make one feel better like Ruskin did. They have such curious manners, too, and may be addicted, for all I know, to drink, or something. At all events one cannot judge a man's work till he is dead. As for your suggested orgies, I should think you might be satisfied with the Pageants that every summer enliven our rural districts."

Then the sad Dionysus of to-day gets wroth with Pentheus, and says to him as he said to him of old:

> Thou dost not see : thou dost not know
> What thou livest, nor who thou art.

He replies now as then:

> I am Pentheus, the son of Agave and Echion,
> I am Hobson the son of Mr. and Mrs. Hobson!

"Alas, poor Pentheus. Happy enough are you feeding on the fat of the land, and oppressing the people so long as the air does not tremble to the faint echo of a madman's song."

"What is this folly?" says Pentheus. "I am a rational being, I have a cultivated imagination, I am a respectable member of society, my religion is the religion of all good men. Leave me in peace."

The poor man is right, he is always right. But his

well-meaning philanthropy is a grim parody of divine goodness; his paltry cruelty a dim reflection of the divine vengeance that may fall on him yet again; his knock-kneed honour is pale before the blazing glory of our faith. His humdrum days may be pleasant or painful; he has never tasted of our purple grapes of heavy sorrow, our golden grapes of super-human joy. Alas, poor Pentheus!

MANSUR

THERE was a Sultan of Turkey who was moved to send a fairly expensive present to the Sultan of China, with this thought in his heart: "There is only one God, and he is all-powerful and all-just, and assuredly I will appoint Mansur to be Captain of the Escort, and to go to China with the present. Mansur will be pleased with the honour, and cease tormenting my ears with his uninteresting tales of oppression in the provinces. It is a long way to China. If this high enterprise succeed, glory will accrue to me, and limitless renown, and a present from the King of China. If it fail, the escort will fertilize the desert of Turkestan, and Mansur with them, peace be on his soul."

Mansur received the command of the Sultan, and prepared to set out from Stamboul with a thousand foot, a hundred horse, and the fairly expensive present. He bade good-bye to Zuleika his wife, and to Ahmad his son, then turned to look for the last time at his books of poetry and prose; and he regretted them with a profound regret. For these books were in Persian, in Arabic, and in Ottoman, and they were written on fine paper of Samarkand by Beber, and Mustafa the son of Qaf and Ashiq of Bagdad; sump-

47

tuous were the tail-pieces and charming the illustrations.
He wandered about the cool library for a full hour,
wandering from shelf to shelf; and he wondered which
should be a fit companion for this long journey. At
last he selected the "Divan of Nesemi," a small volume,
written and painted by Mustafa the son of Qaf. The
story of Nesemi is this:

He was a lord among the Ottomans, wealthy,
powerful, and secure. But he bowed his head to the
teaching of Fazl Ullah the heretic, upon whom descend
God's wrath, and his punishment here was less than
his punishment to come. Thereupon he rejected his
dignity and looked askance at power; and when he
had transferred all his wealth to his son, he set out to
wander and to be a Calender, he and Khandan his
brother. One day he slept under the stars, and dreamt,
and woke up shouting: "I am the Truth, I am God!"
Whereupon he ran to the next village, stood in the
market-place bareheaded to the morning sun, and
shouted: "I am the Truth, I am God." Many of the
villagers laughed at him, but some changed their hue
to yellow for the greatness of their fear, and cried:
"A Blasphemer!" Then Khandan came in pursuit of
his brother and called to him: "Remember the fate of
Fazl Ullah." Nesemi said: "Why do you speak to
God?" Khandan smiled, and after a little thought
recited this couplet:

> Disclose to none the secret word,
> Nor feed with sweets the vulgar herd.

But Nesemi answered at once:

The ocean to its floor is stirred
When we pronounce that holy word.
The bright beloved dwells on high,
And shall the lover tell a lie?

and he continued to shout "I am God" until the
police came and dragged him before the Mufti of
Aleppo. His poems were cited as evidence in court,
and when the Mufti had heard them as far as the first
half of the first Ghazel, he plucked at his beard and
cried: " Enough! Flay him at once." So four disgusting negroes seized him, stripped him, bound him, and
sharpened their knives on his back, and made incisions,
and began to flay him downwards from the shoulders
with leisurely movements and the extreme of satisfaction. The Mufti observed: " A foul death for a foul
fellow; he reeks of pollution. If a drop of his blood
should fall on to a limb it were well to cut that limb
off." At that instant a drop of Nesemi's blood spurted
out and alighted on the Mufti's little finger. " Salaam
to your little finger," observed Khandan, who was
awaiting his turn to be flayed. " In exemplification is
no evil," quoted the Mufti: "and this is an example
and no case." Nesemi heard and said:

God will preserve from all untimely knocks
The little fingers of the Orthodox.
Come, flay the Heretic from top to toe!
He will not weep: he will not make a show.

Khandan said: "Well turned, my brother!" Nesemi
said: "Who talks to God? I am God:" and bowed
his head in anguish, and breathed out the vital

E

spark. But his punishment hereafter is worse. This is the story of Nesemi.

After putting the Divan of Nesemi into his turban, Mansur set out at the head of his hundred horsemen and thousand foot; and they streamed out of the city like an enchanted river, and the present was with them. They journeyed towards the East two months. However, when they came to the borders of India, the King of India, who was an infidel heathen, sent an army against them. They were defeated, and many died, and others became slaves never to return; and Mansur escaped alone and on foot. They say that the King of India was rather pleased with the fairly expensive present that the Sultan of Turkey had intended for the Sultan of China, but our tale is of Mansur. He wandered from well to well among the deserted villages of that hot and warlike land, subsisting on radishes which those who came to wash the radishes had let fall in the well-houses; and he gathered the fruits of unfamiliar trees. One day he came to an inhabited village, and asked for food by signs. They refused it, but did not harm him; only some officials came and took away his embroidered coat and the Divan of Nesemi, which still lay in his turban; and they could not read it, but he knew it by heart. Mansur left that village, not knowing which way to turn, and for a moment he wanted to die; but life is sweet. So he trudged along a dusty path towards the uplands, singing aloud from his lost Divan a song that voyagers love:

Nesemi comprehends not fear, though Drouth and Dark and
    Death be near;
He drank at the primeval feast the mellow draught of Unity.
A traveller with staff in hand he wanders through a ghostly
    land,
And wonders who is at his side, guiding his footsteps lovingly.
The Master's face is Light of Light, his hair is Mystery of
    Night:
With Musa I behold the Sight, a Sinai in verity.
My body is the holy glass where eighteen thousand aeons
    pass:
I talk the language of the stars, I hold the secret of the sea.

He sang till his throat became too dry for singing, and at the time of blazing noon he came to yet another deserted well. Here he found to his sorrow that the bucket had fallen into the well, so he tied a rag to the dangling rope and sucked the moisture that it gathered—a slender satisfaction. So he took off his shoe, tied it to the rope, and let it down into the well. But the rope broke, and his shoe fell into the water. He tied the other shoe on to the rope, and drew it up safely and drank with eagerness and joy. Then he looked about for some refuse to eat, but since he found none, he sat down, and tried to make two shoes out of one. In the end the work tired him, and he looked up and saw a young man before him, nor could the beauty of the young man be described, for all that he was clothed in rags and seemed a little faint with the heat. The young man said to Mansur: "Salaam to you, and the peace of God," and he said it after the manner and in the speech of the Muslims. Mansur replied quietly: "And to you the Salaam." He was drowsy with weariness and sunshine, and he disbelieved in this tall young man who spake to him in the sweet language of his faith. "I am a wayfarer and a stranger," said Mansur. "So am I," said the youth, and without another word he tied the can he had with him on to the rope, and let it down into the well and drew water. Mansur looked eagerly at the can, for he was thirsty again. "Have patience," said the lad, opening his wallet, and drawing out of it some fried peas and a little rice. This he shared with Mansur, and gave him water to drink. He then asked Mansur who he was; and Mansur replied: "I am Mansur of Stamboul, the Ottoman; and who are you?" The young man replied: "My name is the Joyful Heart: will you be my companion?" "Willingly and obediently," said Mansur, "but tell me whence you come and whither you go." The stranger replied: "I am the Joyful Heart; it is time for us to pursue our way." On this Mansur tried to rise from the ground, but he could not stand; so he sat down and said to the stranger: "I could walk before you came; now I am unable." "Get on my back and put your arms round my neck," said the stranger. "You are not strong enough for this work," said Mansur. The stranger laughed and said: "God will make the strength of one suffice for two." He stooped and easily lifted Mansur on to his back, and bade him say "God is my Protector, and there is no refuge but in Him." So Mansur kept repeating these words dreamily, as he travelled along the dusty path on the back of Joyful Heart, till he fell asleep. When he awoke he no more had his arms round the young man's neck, but was lying against a wall in the street of some great city, as ragged and unnoticed as a beggar. He heard the cries of those who sold their wares and the intimate speech of passers-by, and seemed to understand the tongue, and opened his eyes. Above him rose a great snowy building; shouting with joy and terror he recognized the dome of the Mosque of Suleyman, the glory of Stamboul.

Mansur returned to his house, and they knew him, and rejoiced to the limit of joy to behold him; and he found his wife faithful and his son despairing for him, and his library swept and dusted. They led him to the bath, and clothed him, and made him a hot supper, and asked him about his tale; and when he told them, they wondered the more, and thanked God for his safety. Immediately he bought another manuscript of the Divan of Nesemi, written on paper of Damascus by Ashiq of Bagdad; and every night he gave a great dinner to his friends, so that he might make them to know his story. Every night his guests heard about the Joyful Heart and the miraculous journey; and every night after hearing it they exclaimed: "God be praised for thy safety, and verily this is the most wonderful of all wonderful tales, and is worthy to be written down in golden ink." Moreover, they brought news to the Sultan of the strange coming of Mansur, and the Sultan bit the tongue of acquiescence with the tooth of regret, and invited him to the palace, concealing his disappointment, and sat him down at his right hand, and heard the story and was amazed, so that when it was ended he cried " By God!" and gave him a hundred dirhems.

Thus did Mansur plunge into the river of delights, and ate his fill from the dish of satisfaction. When he tired of telling his adventure to his friends, and of entertaining them, he betook himself to his books. He read the "Khosrev and Shirin" of Sheykhi and the tale of Iskander, which Hamedi wrote in a hundred thousand lines, and he became unhappy, and the road of Life was dark before his eyes. And the poets have said:

> My satisfaction cloys to-day, and brings me bitter pain:
> Purge me with colocynth, I pray: I tire of sugar-cane.

But Mansur was longing for the Joyful Heart, and for his companionship. So he departed into the country, and drank wine, and lay down in a meadow, and took out the book of Nesemi, opening it by chance; and he read this quatrain:

> Amazing boy, rise with the dawn, and pour
> The ruby in the crystal. Would you store
> These stolen minutes in a mortal home
> And seek them afterwards, and find no more?

Now when he read this verse he wept, and the wine lay heavy on his soul, and he prepared to sleep. But even as he bowed his head for slumber there came a gentle voice to him, saying "Salaam!" Looking up, he saw the Joyful Heart, dressed in rags, and a little tired with the heat. "Will you be my companion?" said Joyful Heart. Then Mansur became like a man who does not know whether he sleep or wake, for he saw all the flowers of the meadow shining in the eyes of Joyful Heart, and he followed him, and was heard of no more.

CANDILLI

THAT there are landscapes whose beauty is intrinsically mournful, I admit; there are summer afternoons in England when the clouds lie low on the horizon, and the shadows of the hedges stretch out over the fields whose loveliness we recognize as sad. But in other lands than England reign endless sunshine and bright colour, and the scene that has met my eyes all to-day should make the veriest dullard dance to behold its radiant joy. I have been staring for hours out of my window to-day, letting my thoughts and glances wander down the cobbled and precipitous street of Candilli, where dog and man lie sleeping, past the village minaret, out across the Bosphorus and all the myriad laughter of the tiny waves, to the further shore where rise the chivalrous old towers of Roumeli Hissar, which men called the Castle of Damalis five hundred years ago. If the world holds a fairer prospect, I, who have wandered a little, have not seen it; yet all its brightness and splendour does but fill my mind with sorrow and unrest. I have been watching for three hours the tracts of warm light on those giant-rounded keeps, and the thousand boats that ply the highway of the salt sea-river, sad I know not why. I have waited till evening, idle in my chair, till the brown Castle walls turned gold, and the blue sea white and wet, till the sun went down not amid the patches and pageantry of our Northern settings, but gently leaving a sky as softly coloured as the petal of a rose: and the lamps were swung high on to the masts of the great ships steaming out to Russia through the gloom. Sick at heart with so much loveliness was I, and then brief twilight came, netting the world in spectral blue, till I cried out for darkness like a cave-beast blinded by the glare. And now darkness is here with her fixed and trailing stars, and the whole European shore is ablaze from Therapia to Stamboul; the Muezzin has cried from his little minaret, the Ottoman night has begun.

Is it unmanly or decadent of me to long for a slag-heap or a gaswork, or any strong, bold, ugly thing to break the spell of this terrible and malignant beauty that saps body and soul? Yet there are few who did not feel what they might call a " touch of sadness " in sweet popular phrase, when first they saw the boundless sea, or mountains capped with snow. The misery I feel lies deep in the nature of man; such thoughts as I am thinking, millions have thought before. For here, it seems, is the very face of Beauty, here one may gaze into her eyes and watch them change. But who am I to enjoy this high gift of the gods? what can I do with it, how make it my own? Why is it there, part of my foolish daily life: can I treat it as a common thing? To deserve, to enjoy this magnificence, a man should have a high work, or at least a noble plan. A poet might sing of it, and find peace;

or a painter paint it; glorious would it shine to a man
returning from a long journey, if among those countless lights one light meant home. Even to me these
scenes were joyful that day I rode over the Anatolian
hills, and the weariness of body banished all sickness
from the mind, and my head was void of fancies, and
I saw little as we cantered along the sandy tracks
save spars of sunlight and flashes of sea. But now,
though my limbs are aching to be up and doing, I am
fascinated by deadly wonder; and he who sinks before this spell sits in his chair for hours and plays with
dreams. He dreams of a mistress as Thais gentle or
as Helen fair, and of the palace one might raise upon
the hill in marble symmetry and store with curious
broideries of the East; and of all that life might be to a
man who conquered it, and why Antony was wise.
And he dreams vain private hopes of his own of
which he is ashamed. And he ponders on the narrow
lane of sea, and of all that ancient histories have told
him; of Sultans and Emperors; he remembers how
the proud flags of Venice once flew splendid in the
breeze, and how the relentless Romans before them
built walls and ways, and how once the little Argo
rounded the point with blue-eyed Jason on her prow,
and the merry, toiling crew, bound on the first adventure of the world. And a light fever distracts the
dreamer's body, and his mind longs for some coercive
chain, and he begins to understand why men of the
East will sit by a fountain from noon to night, and
let the world roll onward.

THE 'BUS IN STAMBOUL

ACROSS the Galata bridge it plies seething with a babel horde; beneath the shadow of the great mosques valiantly it rumbles on, till their spacious domes re-echo, and the lily minarets are all a-tremble; right into the secret ways of Stamboul it travels, the bright red motor-'bus. Weary was I of the long streets and the dust, and the endless sun of Constantinople's fierce July, I could not face the jostling on the Galata bridge. I took the motor-'bus.

I sat down next to a very fat Turk, whose face betrayed an intellectual curiosity alien to his nature. I followed the perplexed glances of his earth-brown eyes. They were turned to an inscription written on the end wall of the 'bus behind the driver, an inscription he could not understand. I looked and thrilled; in fair letters, plain for all to see, they stared at me those golden words, those names of places half forgotten and long desired, Oxford Circus, Marble Arch, Edgware Road, and Cricklewood.

Thus, like a chime of silver, distant bells, or some sweet poem of a fickle lover who has strung together the names of his mistresses and loves, whispers in my ear this table of fares in the old Vanguard motor-'bus, till I could weep for the bitterness of my exile and my great desire for London Town and English faces;

for the thunder of Charing Cross and the cries of Oxford Circus, for the sweep of Regent Street and the motors of Piccadilly, for the glory of a great Empire and the fellowship of men.

And you, too, O Cricklewood, lovely Cricklewood of the idle evenings, not so far from Hampstead Heath, Cricklewood, where clerks, returning from toil, eat their suppers and kiss their young wives, and sleep at peace with God and all the world, you are worth all the golden East, obscure and lovely Cricklewood, whatever those literary men say—and forget it not. Within your walls, brave Cricklewood, had you but walls, would be found more enlightenment and knowledge, more true learning and humanity than in all this bright imperial city, age-worn, battered, bejewelled, prostitute of East and West, which you now supply, O wealthy Cricklewood, with your superfluous means of transport.

Robinson, of Cricklewood, incipient banker, citizen of the greatest city the world has ever known, I fear you have forgotten this 'bus, and how it would ever and anon break down in Maida Vale, and leave you impatient and angry on the pavement in the rain. ("Passengers are requested not to put their wet mackintoshes on the seats," it is still up there over the window. Well, there *was* a shower here last month now I come to think of it.) Ah well, they travel on, these old Vanguards and Pioneers : they will go farther yet. For they say that two of them were unshipped at Beirout the other day, to be sent up country, to Bagdad.

C/ple, July, 1910.

TRANSLATIONS FROM THE GULISTAN

I

ONE of the Kings of Khorassan saw in a dream Sultan Mahmud, who had been dead for a hundred years. Though all the rest of his body had crumbled into dust his eyes still rolled and stared in their bony habitations. The wiseacres were at a loss to interpret this, but a Dervish threw light on the problem, and remarked, " A stranger has usurped his power and state: no wonder that his eyes are animate."

Since deep and dark an ancient host unheeded and unknown
    remains,
Since earth exerts her uttermost, till not one single bone
    remains,
Since of the great Nushirovan the history alone remains,
Lead a delightful life, O man, for nothing, when that's flown,
    remains.

II

A king had a Persian slave with him on board ship who had not set eyes on the sea before, and had never experienced the discomforts of navigation. The lad wept and wailed and began to shake all over; to verbal consolations he would pay no attention, and he entirely damped the king's enjoyment. However, a doctor who was there said: "Your majesty, if you permit, I will set the lad on the road of silence;" said the monarch, "I should esteem it a favour." On this the doctor ordered the boy to be flung into the sea. He accordingly received a sound ducking; but at length they took hold of his hair and drew him to the side of the ship. The unfortunate slave clung tight to the rudder, scrambled on to the deck and sat down in a corner without a word. The delighted king exclaimed: "What doctoring is this?" The leech replied, "Formerly the lad had no experience of drowning and its horrors, and undervalued the safety of the ship, but now he rejoices in that safety even as convalescents rejoice in health."

> The epicure rejects the loaf that satisfies the pauper's need.
> You think the lady ugly, Sir? I think her very nice indeed.
> Though purgatory seem as foul as Hell itself to angel eyes,
> I guess the people down below think Purgatory Paradise.

III

They tell the story of an offensive person who hit a dervish on the head with a stone. The holy man, having no opportunity of revenge, put the stone by. After a time the king let loose the battalions of his wrath against the offensive person, and clapped him into the lowest pit of the dungeon. One day the dervish came along and flung that stone at his head. "Who are you?" asked the prisoner, "and why did you fling that stone at my head?" The good man replied; "I am so and so; this is the very stone that on such and such a date you flung at mine." "Where have you been all this time?" inquired the prisoner. The other replied:

"Fright at your rank has turned into delight at your disaster: and wags have said:

While evil men were fortunate the wise were not importunate,
They had no claws to tear and scratch, they did not want a
    fighting match.
Anguish the silver wrist will feel, that grapples with a fist of
    steel,
But when your foe is bound in chains, how easy to beat out his
    brains?

IV

Once I breathed and moved in a company of young enthusiasts on the way to Meccah; we used to hum as we marched along, or intone a spiritual hymn. There was with us a hermit who disapproved of our dervish manners, and made light of our penitence and pain. But when we came to the palm grove of the son of Hulal

There came a dusky Arab boy who raised a voice so splendid,
That all the denizens of air hung in the air suspended.

Then I remarked that the camel which that surly eremite bestrode began to prance and dance till it flung that holy man and disappeared into the desert. Said I : " Sir, your camel has run away in an ecstasy : can you remain unmoved ? "

Before the dawn began to pale, I heard the golden nightingale :
"O base and brutish heart !" he cried, " If love is never to
    prevail !
Hearing that sweet Arabian lad your camel rose and danced
    like mad ;
If you don't care you ought to wear a snout in front, behind a
    tail."

V

I saw a pious man sitting by the shore of the sea. He had been wounded by a tiger, and could find no medicine for his case. And yet he never ceased praising glorious Almighty God. They asked him : " Why do you render thanks ? " He replied, " God be praised that I have a pain in my body not a stain on my soul ! "

> If I were doomed to die by that dear Friend,
> I gladly would comply and face my end ;
> But if he said " I am not pleased with thee,"
> Then I instead would miserable be.

VI

A godly man had a dream in which he saw a king in paradise and a monk in hell. " Now why," said he to himself, " is the king by choirs contented and the monk by fires tormented ? for I expected the con-

verse." There came to him a voice, saying: " The
king is here because of his affection for monks; the
monk there because of his connection with kings."

> Where is the use of frock and staff and cowl
> If words be foolish or if deeds be foul?
> Deal justly, Sir, and lay your hymn-book down,
> The righteous man keeps righteous in a crown.

VII

In an hour of great distress a dervish stole a rug
from a friend of his. "Cut off his hand," said the
Judge. The owner of the rug himself pleaded for the
prisoner whom, he declared, he had entirely forgiven.
The Judge said to him: " I cannot abate the rigour of
the law at your request." " A just pronouncement,"
came the answer, "yet we need not punish those
who steal from a charity fund; a dervish am I, too,
and all my property is devoted to the poor." The
Judge found this reasonable and pardoned the thief,
but before letting him go he reprimanded him,
saying: " Is the world so narrow that you had to
victimize a friend?" The culprit replied: " My lord,
have you not heard the saying: 'Sweep the floor of
your friend: fly the door of your foe.'"

> When the days of want begin, do not let disaster in:
> Rob your comrade of his jacket and your rival of his skin.

VIII

One of the Saintly saw a big man wild with passion and foaming at the mouth, and asked what was the matter. Someone replied: "He is suffering from an opprobrious epithet." "Why," rejoined the Saint, "he could carry a ton of bricks; can't he bear a mocking word?

> Weak of will and intellect
> Do you think that men who place
> Fists in their opponent's face
> Win approval or respect?

said the Saint, and after a pause he continued:

> Though their arms be adamant
> Though they scalp an elephant,
> Men without humanity
> Seem contemptible to me.

FORGOTTEN WARFARE

THE first of my trivial tales—and trivial indeed they seem in these mighty days of conflagration —has for scene Beyrout, that Syrian port as well known to the pilgrims in collars who seek Jerusalem as to those without who prefer Mecca. Here, one spring morning, the report of a cannon—a single and extremely noisy shot of warning—roused me from sleep. The dreaded Italians had come. That Roman land had sent two fine cruisers to sink a Turkish gunboat (lately repaired in Genoa) small enough for either of them to have hoisted on deck and used as a launch, and there they were, by Jove, flying their battle-flags just outside my window!

Soon after, the fun began. The Italians sent five shells over the town by mistake, and one each through two banks. About a hundred interested spectators on the quay, struck by the bursting shells, paid the penalty of their rashness. As for the Turks, no watch had been kept on the boat; the officers all slept on shore and only a few reached the ship 'in time. But they refused to surrender and pluckily mis-directed several shells all round the harbour, till their little biscuit tin was sunk up to its funnels. The attempt made by some gallant Arab boatmen to sink the cruisers by rifle fire failed completely. They had been persuaded, ever since the day of the *Camperdown* disaster off Tripoli in Syria, that you had only to puncture an ironclad and it would disappear.

Meanwhile, in the centre of the town, things were, as the French say, "well otherwise serious." At the first shots the Arabs fled howling indoors in senseless panic; recovering, they looted the barracks and attempted to murder all Christians, myself included, and the Governor only just succeeded in restoring order at the risk of his life. He placed himself at the head of some twenty soldiers against a violent mob intent on breaking open the prisons and liberating all the vilest riff-raff to help in the looting. As for me, an extremely unpleasant crowd, having just succeeded in looting rifles from the barracks, stopped my carriage, and, sticking their bayonets uncomfortably near my stomach, swore I was the Italian Consul. I said no, but that I was a splendid Englishman. At that moment the cannon of the cruisers began to roar again, making everyone more excited and dangerous than ever. I cocked my revolver in my pocket determined to shoot through my coat at one particularly horrid fat man. But that moment deliverance came from an excellent Turkish soldier, who, leaping on to the step of the carriage, and turning his rifle on the crowd, bade drive on to the hotel, which I reached safely.

There, on my return, I found a Mahommedan friend of mine—one of those admired Young Turks who have read Herbert Spencer, Mallarmé, and

Sherlock Holmes, and thereby become renowned for their liberal tendencies and Parisian culture. He, not knowing I was somewhat sore upon the point, explained to me in great excitement, and with ancestral fanaticism blazing from his eyes, that a massacre of Christians (or at least of his fellow subjects, the *native* Christians) was now not only inevitable, but a mere measure of obvious justice.

It was a paltry affair of a few hours, but while it lasted it seemed like the end of the world. Unforgetable the thunder of the guns shaking the golden blue of sky and sea, while not a breath stirred the palm trees, not a cloud moved on the swan-like snows of Lebanon.

.   .   .   .   .

This was not the only occasion on which the Italians offered us good sport at Beyrout, and again the inhabitants played up fine. It was summer now, and in summer the happy Beyroutins have the pleasure of sleeping on the cool spurs of Lebanon, and the anguish of being hoisted up and down at a walking pace in the rack-and-pinion railway. The Lebanon, one may remind the reader, is a privileged land with a Christian Governor; while Beyrout is a sort of island of pure Turkey. One morning, very early, warships were descried off the harbour. Is it the foe again, or only the frequently protective French? That is the question debated at Aley station by the anxious crowd waiting to descend to town. An ascending train puts all doubt to rest; fugitives are sitting on the roof; the Italians are here again. The Beyroutins decided to remain on the mountains; we descended almost alone. And here it may be observed that when Levantines (as in this case) act with perfect common sense and prudence the Europeans of the place always call them cowards; or, when they prefer to look on some dangerous spectacle unperturbed, or to arm to defend their liberties, they instantly call them fools.

However, there was no trouble. No European town could have behaved better. On the quays a mixed crowd, secretly armed, for certain, in the Oriental way, watched a boat packed with Italian bluejackets and sporting a single brass cannon in the bow, examine the ships in the port, and that testimony to their comrades' valour, the sunken Turkish gunboat, and made no demonstration whatever.

Thinking my duty done, I took the train back to the mountain. But the East is the father of surprises! All the Lebanese I saw from the carriage windows were openly armed; while their women and children who fled Beyrout this morning were rushing down again to face the Arab or Italian peril. On my arrival home I found in front of my cottage a little squadron of Lebanese cavalry prancing before the door. Entering, I discovered two American lady missionaries from the neighbouring village of Abadieh who, having received a very large bullet in their drawing-room, had taken refuge with my wife.

It seemed it was all those wicked Druses again! A much respected old gentleman of their tribe had been grievously wounded by a hand unknown on his way from Brumana; hence the Druses were assembling in their secret places crying for Christian blood; and hence the Christians of the valley, led by some brawny returned emigrants from America, had had all the church bells rung as a summons to all Christians to gather in force. A good scrap is still considered to be better than litigation in the Lebanon—and, after all, what is Lebanese Justice unless you've got a consul to doctor your case? A woman accused of stealing a hen will fly to Russia or France for protection. A Druse appeals to England, who once preserved them from richly merited punishment at the hands of the French for their massacring ways. The English public was persuaded by a venal press that a Druse was a kind of Protestant suffering martyrdom at the hands of papistical Maronites.

But if England protects she must also restrain, and the duty of ending this nonsense obviously fell on the British Consul-General, who accomplished it with all the skill of one accustomed to Oriental incidents. First he persuaded the Christians to remain on the defensive. Then we drove to Abadieh. The moonlight was streaming in the enormous rocky gorge of the Beyrout river; and here and there a Lebanese gendarme set to guard the road started up from some dark corner into the white glow to salute us—his strange costume so fantastic in the moonlight that the whole scene seemed to stiffen into cardboard, and one waited to hear the music of some absurd Oriental opera by Hérold or Rossini. There were few enough of these gendarmes, and they would have had a poo show if the Druses had risen in earnest. Vividly the moon shone now on Abadieh, on the little fortress-like houses, on the runic carvings of an old Druse tomb, mysterious beneath a splendid chestnut tree, and on the worn brown stones and red tiles of the old courtyard where we halted. In Syria you can see colours quite distinctly by the light of a full moon. We were admitted and welcomed at the narrow door; and first of all paid a brief visit to the wounded old gentleman who had caused all the trouble. He lay there very cheerful on pink and green cushions suggestive of the Mahommedan Paradise. Then, while the Consul worked hard at conciliation, I talked amiably with the lesser notables. They were still undecided about that massacre, and they had enjoyed themselves greatly shooting about all day at nothing in particular (hence the little accident to the missionaries' house); but, as they would never have dreamt of massacring us, conversation on the usual Syrian topics—" What will the Italians do? What will the French do?"—flowed comfortably. The whole affair was soon brilliantly settled by the Consul-General, and, the wildest spirits having been calmed, we drove home by midnight.

What utter foolery is enough to start a massacre in the East! But let no injustice be done to the Lebanon. Its security in the last fifty years has, after all, been never seriously troubled. Laugh at its botched-up Government if you will, and then remember that it possesses the only countryside in the Turkish Empire, the southern environs of Constantinople excepted, where you can enjoy a picnic without the presence of an armed guard, and even let the governess take the children for a walk alone.

.   .   .   .   .   .

Some months after I saw the smoke and heard the distant rumble of the battle of Lemnos—the one effort made by the Turks to secure the mastery of the Ægean.

A pretty sight it had been that morning to pass the Turkish fleet, cleared for action and lined across the entrance to the Dardanelles, while a little destroyer spluttered up from the west to give them news of the foe. It was one of those indescribable winter days on the Ægean, with a hot sun and a piping breeze : the water was all laced blue and silver, and the windmills of Tenedos whirled fit to break. "Tenedos dives opum," quoted to me the new Armenian Governor of Lebanon, to my great pleasure ; yet how can the place ever have been rich ? I agreed it was strange—that little windy rock looks as if it had never produced anything more planturous than stonecrop since the Creation.

We were near Mytilene when we heard the guns. Thrilling enough it was to me—fired with the glory that *is* Greece—this fight against the Unspeakable for that Greek and Christian sea. Not so, however, to the trio of American ladies aboard—for all that they were on their devout way from Athens to Jerusalem. Impossible to make these pious folk understand that Greece and Christianity were no mere phantoms of the past, but were still alive, and, with excellent guns, even kicking.

At last, in despair of awaking interest, and hoping to horrify, I said to one of them: " But men are killing each other over there, you know!"

She put up her eyeglass at me.

" *Nonsense!* " she said, and walked down to lunch.

We were soon gliding through the beautiful Strait of Mytilene. As we passed the little town buried in olive groves, with its mediaeval castle all on a green lawn, a great Greek flag waved proudly over the scene, its colours blending with the blue and white waves so finely that it was impossible to imagine the Turkish scarlet in its place. As we neared the harbour we slowed down, and a lot of rough-looking pirates came rowing out and shouted to an old Greek priest on board for news.

The old Papas replied that he had only heard noise; had only seen smoke.

" That's all right! " said they, " it's a glorious victory! "—and bang! bang! bang! went their revolvers into the windy void.

And, after all, so it was.

. . . . . .

To think that it was with cheerful anecdotes like these that I had hoped, a white-haired elder, to impress my grand-children! Now there's not a peasant from Picardy to Tobolsk but will cap me with tales of real and frightful tragedy. What a race of deep-eyed and thoughtful men we shall have in Europe after the war—now that all those millions have been baptized in fire! But for my little memories I can keep at least this distinction—the unearthly beauty of the East. I mean the adjective. A man may find Naples or Palermo merely pretty; but the deeper violet, the splendour and desolation of the Levant waters is something that drives into the soul.

PHILANTHROPISTS

MY heart goes black with fury and horror when I read their Wills. The only consolation one has is that there is another of them dead. Ten thousand pounds to the Wigan Home for Cats, five thousand to the Society for the Suppression of Sunday Amusements, a thousand for the Syrian Lunatic Asylum on Mount Lebanon, and fifty pounds a year (altered by a pencil-stroke to twenty-five) for their old and faithful clerk, Mr. Jinks.

One knows that the philanthropist himself, for all his riches, got nothing out of life but a sense of his own importance. It was he who once prevented Maud Allan dancing in Manchester, and it was he who made Manchester. He never travelled except to Lucerne or Nice. Yet he had enough money to have wandered round the world. He might have stood on the slope of Tanagra, and seen the reflection of the snow-topped mountains of Euboea glide like swans on the still blue waters of the Euripus. He might have floated down the Tigris from Mosul to Bagdad in a raft of skins and been potted by Arabs from the bank. He might have walked beneath heavy Indian skies and understood in a flash, standing in the monstrous shadow of an ancient god, the secret of all

Empires. He might have smoked opium with dim Chinese and travelled in his dreams right out of the world to starry isles and planetary oceans. He did none of these things.

If he really preferred to stay at home he might have tried to learn something about the noble pleasures of life. He might have discovered why some men still read poetry and some still write it! He might have helped some poor devil of a struggling author to publish his works, or backed some play a little too good for the British stage. He might have appreciated art or music. But Mendelssohn's " Elijah " was the high water-mark of his artistic comprehension. Blair Leighton was good enough for his walls. Poetry he left to his women-folk, who strewed the works of Ella Wheeler Wilcox and Mr. Alfred Noyes on their drawing-room tables, and were thought to be cultured. He did not even build himself a fine house in the country to perpetuate his memory. He did not impress his personality on a garden or a terrace. He lived in a house with an area and great shutterless windows like blank lifeless eyes.

" But," say you, " if he was a quiet, decent, stay-at-home sort of man, what does it all matter? If he were a true Christian, if he made those around him happy and contented, small need of art or travel to justify his existence! " Well, he never drank, he never flirted, he never sang, he smoked a little (thank God!), he was just (in a way) to his clerks, rather brutal to his son, rather stupidly indulgent to his daughters, who despised his absence of culture. His wife died young.

As he was rich, men were apt to say he killed her. In any case she was of the South Country. It cannot be said he made anybody strikingly happy while he lived. The worst of it is, he made so very few happy when he died.

Was it his fault? He did try in his Will at least to "do some good" and to purchase by large bequests to colourless institutions a sufficient mansion in the Kingdom of Heaven. This thing and that thing seemed worthy of support—seemed to be vaguely beneficial. He had no disinterested person to advise him. He was not a bad fellow at heart—if he had a heart.

Perhaps some other plutocrat will read this and say: "Tell us now, if you had some money, young man, which you never will have, since money needs character to obtain and still more character to hold, how would you leave it in your Will apart from bequests to your family? We men of business are, I think, more likely than you to know how to spend money for charity as for anything else. We give and bequeath to sound institutions of proved utility and unimpeachable character. How will you better that?" Let me give him a straight answer. Let me sketch out my last Will and Testament, as it would appear if I were rich.

Well, first of all, £10,000 would be administered by my friend S. (on whose judgment I can rely) for the publication of jolly or sound poetry: also to be used as a travelling fund to take promising young authors on a holiday to Corfu, where there are no social problems, and everyone is just as perfectly happy and

poor as this life allows. I would also bequeath £5,000
(would I had it in the world!) to the excellent Society
founded by friends of Ruskin, that preserves some of
England's scenery from smoke, filth, and modern
architecture. There, if you like, is an unimpeachable
institution! A little carved stone might be stuck up
to serve as a stile from field to field and to declare
"James Flecker saved this little view from the Van-
dals." Then I might leave £10 to some favourite
author—say to Mr. Max Beerbohm, "from a total
stranger who enjoyed 'Zuleika Dobson,'" to buy
a case of Port to drink to the immortality of
Oxford.

I don't mean by this and my other bequest that
everyone should fill their Wills with bequests to
authors. This is my Will, and I'm a reading man,
and I do think reading men forget to recognize those
who give them pleasure far too completely.

Leave to your own guild. If you are a consul,
don't forget the fellow in your service that went
smash; if a doctor, think of the poor fellow struggling in a slum practice even if you don't know him.
If you are no one in particular, imitate my last
bequest. Thus it runs:

"£1,000 each to John Tubbs, greengrocer, Mary
Alison, a typewriter girl, Robert Johns, bank clerk,
Mr. and Mrs. Curver and Miss Black."

Who, you ask, are Mr. Tubbs and the rest of them?
No, they none of them saved my life from drowning,
nor are they (as far as I know) mute Miltons or un-
hung McWhirters. They are just some rather decent

people in what are called "straitened circumstances." I got the names of some of them from the old Vicar. When they hear about their legacies they will be unable to believe their ears. They will be struck all of a heap. Life will suddenly become a fairy tale for them. They will be, I hope, delirious for joy. They won't know what to do with the money. Some will spend it wisely and some foolishly, and some, I hope, will marry on it, and some married already will take their children to the seaside. The Philanthropic Institution did not dance when it got its thousand pounds from the Philanthropist. It was merely " gratified to announce the fact." But John Tubbs will dance, perhaps with Mary Alison! I shall not have left my money to institutions that " may perhaps do some good after all." I shall have certainly made some poor devils happy. And that is what Christ meant by charity.

For years Englishmen have been puzzled by the difference between Charity and Philanthropy. This War has come to help them. War is a great eye-opener all round. When the public saw figures, well-known for their charitable donations, rushing mountains of goods home in their motor cars, they *did* open their eyes. It's a wonder they didn't open the cars. Then when still more distinguished Philanthropists gave a thousand pounds to the Prince of Wales' Fund and dismissed one hundred employees to make up their loss and a little over, the man in the street, usually long-suffering as a Neapolitan donkey, did violently, and like a spirited horse, protest. Philanthropy was found out at last. The average man has now realized that though many philanthropists are honest, well-intentioned, even noble-minded men, philanthropy itself is a rich man's conspiracy and in the long run a total fraud.

There should be just one philanthropist in a country —and that's the State itself. I'm not talking socialism. I only mean that when charity, which is a personal thing, is organized on so vast a scale as to lose all personal interest or appeal, it is time the State controlled its institutions. Much better the country squire should look after his sick with personal interest and avoid Boards and Committees. But the vast burden of supporting our indispensable London hospitals should be, if not undertaken, at least organized and controlled by the State. Here again the War is making us think. It's obviously right for the women to knit socks. It's obviously right for Lord Roberts to ask me to give my saddle if I have one—because I can have the real pleasure of thinking of the gallant soldier who gets it, blessing its excellence after a hard ride in France. (When you come to think of it, Charity is only of ethical value when it gives pleasure to the giver!) But when one's asked for half sovereigns in aid of some vague distress one gives more reluctantly, and rightly so. One may know the charity's sound, and one supports it ; but one feels all the time how much jollier it would be to give a tramp a meal or to have a Belgian as one's guest. But the great point we are all beginning to realize is that the State seems to have left to vague charitable organization a lot of work which it ought to undertake or at least superintend itself.

This thrilling, this excellent, this tragic War is a great Schoolmaster. May we profit by its lessons. At all events Lesson No. 1 is over. Philanthropy is dead!

II

THE GRECIANS

THE GRECIANS[1]

A DIALOGUE ON EDUCATION

PREFACE

IN a technical matter such as education only the experienced seem to me to have a right to speak. For this reason only, I think it worth while mentioning that I was educated in one public school, and have lived most of my life in another; that I passed four years at Oxford and two at Cambridge, and that it has been my duty as civil servant to learn some eight or nine modern languages. Literature I have practised and art I have studied, but my chief claim to the kind attention of my readers is, after all, that I myself have been many times and in many places a schoolmaster.

I have tried to make this dialogue resemble real conversation, and have aimed at abruptness, vigour, and compression rather than at rounded periods and exact arrangement of subjects. And this I mention in case any reader, offended by a merely artistic violence of language, may imagine it expressive of thoughtlessness or lack of sincerity on the part of the Author.

The British Consulate,
    Constantinople,
        September, 1910.

[1] Reprinted by kind permission of Messrs. J. M. Dent and Sons, Ltd.

CHAPTER I

THE THREE ENGLISHMEN

OUTSIDE Bologna, that old and wise city, rises a little hill with a large prospect called San Michele. The bends of the zigzag path which leads to the summit of this so magnificent hill are embellished with delectable arbours, where fat babies play and their young nurses sleep during the long drowsy evenings of late summer. Such an evening I would have you imagine. Picture to yourself the babies engaged in innocent diversions, the little nurses wandering with princely lovers in the forests of their dreams.

Suddenly a tremendous trampling startled those gentle souls. A little man with hair and beard of that ferocious orange colour which we call red, with iron-rimmed spectacles bobbing on his nose, and a heavy gold watch-chain swaying against his chest, was thundering up the hill as though it had been the Matterhorn and he an enthusiast for records. A sight to make babies cry and nursemaids laugh was Henry Hofman; and strange were the clothes of Henry Hofman, his black trousers, his Norfolk jacket, and his green tie. " Funny man!" said the babies in Italian. " Pazzo inglese!" replied the nursemaids, and slept again. Hofman paid no attention; intent on higher things, he crashed through a row of trees

and attained the top. Then might you have seen him
stalk to the parapet, wave his arms round his head
with fervour and delight, and slap himself on the chest.
" Grand ! " he cried. " Magnificent ! " he shouted, and
had he been, as his father was, a German, he would
have added, " Kolossal ! " Then, arms folded, foot on
parapet, absurd and twisted body silhouetted against
the eternal sky, he stood, he gazed, he exulted.

It was only the view over Bologna and the plain
that had called forth his admiration. After all, few
men are epicures in prospects. All healthy persons
will climb to see a view, and it takes little to thrill
these aesthetic gluttons, provided the weather be clear
and they can see plenty at one time. For no regions
of this world are totally unpleasing when viewed from
an eminence. Henry Hofman had seen a hundred
landscapes finer than this ; yet this was fair enough.
A hundred miles of silver plain reflected the fitful
shadows of the clouds ; a faint blue haze hid and
hinted the Adriatic Sea ; and the peculiar quiet fire
of sunset deepened to crimson the cheerful red of
Bologna's roofs, and shone right through the little
windows of the two great towers that dominate the
city. Let us leave him gazing at the Torre degli
Asinelli and consider a companion of his who has just
arrived, a very bad second. This grizzled, middle-
aged man of uncertain aspect presents something of a
contrast to Hofman. We note the newcomer's rather
fine features, marred by an incessant frown ; we
approve the decent obscurity and neutral tint of his
clothes. His raiment well brushed, without style or

flair, seems to be like its wearer, to be something to which no one could reasonably object. His method of walking, moreover, is unobtrusive; his voice, as he exclaims, " Here we are, Hofman!" is not annoyingly brusque or strident, but verges on a mellow cheerfulness. Yet beneath the contrast which these two men present lurks resemblance; and the indefinable, ineradicable stamp of a great profession marks both those pairs of weary and watchful eyes.

" Ah, it's grand! " shouted Hofman, " grand! Only three days ago I was taking my horrible chemistry class, and now I am on a hill, looking at this!"

He swept his arm round parallel to the horizon.

" Ah, those boys, indeed," said Edwinson, quietly. "Yes, it is pleasant to be free of them for a little— yet I am fond of them, very fond of them. At my age I couldn't give it up; I couldn't do anything else but teach. It's dull work, our trade of instruction; but there are times when I feel it's rather a grand work. Now this city, Hofman, is the foster-mother of education. Bologna has one of the oldest universities of Europe. Teaching in those days must have been much more delightful, when each new book read was a new country explored, and each pupil taught was a new friend won. What a beautiful city it is with all those useless, insolent, aspiring towers—so like Oxford in a way, and so emblematic of that profitless, beautiful training of the mind we try to give."

" So like the education you mediaevalists try to give," grunted Hofman. " I have to teach facts. But it's getting late and dark."

"And all the ways are shadowy," broke in Edwinson, quoting the stock translation of Homer. " And I am hungry. Let us go down to the city and eat."

So saying the unobtrusive Edwinson took his companion's arm, a thing he had never done before during their six years of common toil, and arm-in-arm they sauntered down the hill.

To explain this unusual, almost emotional, impulse on the part of Edwinson, we must remark that it was the first visit of these two men to Italy. Indeed it was their first day in the country if we exclude the inevitable halt in dreary northern Milan. True, they had been twice abroad together before; they had been for one walking tour in Brittany, and one in the Black Forest. But as a rule Hofman spent his winter holidays with his people at Gospel Oak and visited a seaside resort—Southsea or Worthing—in summer. With equal regularity Edwinson retired to Hampstead, or in the bright season of the year took some of his more brilliant and attractive pupils with him for a reading party in Devonshire. This Italian journey had been a bold venture, meticulously pre-arranged. Expenses, routes, second-class fares had been calculated with nicety and a Baedeker; and there had been much diligent self-teaching in a tongue which Hofman found hard and learnt thoroughly and Edwinson found easy and mastered ill. The whole thing was an Event. Events are rare in the pedagogic life.

When they reached the walls of Bologna—Italian cities are still walled—they took a tram which passed along the endless lovely arcaded streets, and brought them back to the vast central square that has its name from Neptune. They had decided against dining at their hotel, and sauntered vaguely along the Via Ugo Bassi to find a suitable place of refreshment—no easy task when sumptuary expense is to be avoided, and cheap squalor shunned. At last they halted, and boldly pushed open a creaking door; for favourable chance had led them to the Toscana. Here in term-time assemble the students of Bologna; here, when there are no students, the modest traveller is welcomed with cordiality and served with dispatch.

They seated themselves, and Edwinson suggested timidly that the wine of the country might be both cheap and good.

"Wine?" said Hofman. "Of course we will drink wine. The water would probably be poisonous."

Their debate was cut short by the arrival of their wine, unbidden, in a shapely wicker-covered flask. Next, at Hofman's unhesitating command, arrived spaghetti (this dish had a lot of local colour, but they found it dull) and veal cutlets alla Milanese, which strong men eat every night; and they ate this and drank enormously of the wine, conversing and laughing without cease.

The restaurant was full; the waiters rushed about; the incessant clatter of spoons and forks and knives on plates, dishes, and glasses was most exhilarating; while expectoration was, for Italy, comparatively rare.

The two friends were only halfway through their

cutlets, when they were disagreeably interrupted by the arrival of a stranger, who hung up a sort of large felt sombrero in such a way as to obscure Hofman's old but comfortable cap, and prepared to sit down beside them. Hofman was bored and, being an honest man, immediately looked what he felt. Edwinson drummed with his fingers on the table.

"I hope you will excuse me," said the stranger to them in pleasant English, "but the place is quite full."

Looking up, they saw before them a young man of elegant figure and handsome appearance, indeed, a remarkably splendid young man. Hofman thought to himself that the new-comer had rather a womanish face. But he ignored the strong chin and resolute thin mouth, and was considering only the complexion. If Hofman had justly realized his own feelings in the matter, he would have found out that he esteemed all beauty a rather womanish thing, unworthy of serious attention. Edwinson, meanwhile, gazed intently on the young man, and since he held the neo-pagan idea of Greece, mentally raved about Apollo. Yet no one could have been more unlike the swarthy, straight-nosed Greeks than this merry-eyed young man, with long, light hair, high cheek bones, and a vivid colouring: no one was less like a lay figure for idealists than this youth with his strong torso and his whimsical and lively countenance. However, Edwinson's admiration of the fascinating stranger even increased when he heard him order special local dishes and wines with an Italian accent so graceful and correct that it seemed far above anything a mere native could possibly have achieved.

By the time the young man turned to look at the two schoolmasters their ill-humour had vanished, and their conversation, instigated by Chianti and an audience, had become more brilliant than ever. To Edwinson returned the fire of his Oxford days: for long ago no one more often than he had sent the sun —and the moon too—to bed with talking. Social qualities, said his friends, had spoilt his chances (never too brilliant, it must be confessed) of academical distinction. Hofman was once more the penurious lad who, in the rare hours snatched from the arduous study of science, used to electrify the Gospel Oak Ethical Club with his incisive wit and outrageous opinions. The stranger put in a word here and there, yet hardly entered into the conversation, but maintained a mysterious though friendly reserve. He vouchsafed nothing about himself, save that his name was Harold Smith, a severe blow to Edwinson, who had imagined him to be of noble parentage.

When the meal was at an end Hofman was so delighted with their new acquaintance that he was preparing to ask him to come and take coffee with them; but he was forestalled by Smith, who leant over towards them, and, in a voice of extreme charm and gentleness, said: "I hope you will do me the favour of coming round to my place: I have a little room of my own in a back street here which we may find a little pleasanter than any café."

They willingly accepted this novel invitation, and

followed their guide through the colonnades of Bologna, whither they knew not. They entered a low and obscure doorway, toiled up a painful stair-case, turned a corner, and found themselves in the sitting-room of Smith. It was a small room, but comfortable beyond all an Italian's dreams, and beautiful enough to satisfy the most exacting of Cambridge aesthetes. A dim, reddish light suggested tapestried hangings, surprising pictures, and innumerable books; yet for all the display of furniture and fabrics in a little space, the room was mysteriously cool. Hofman, turning his eyes to the bookshelves, as reading men will, was delighted to find his beloved moderns, Teutonic and Scandinavian, bound in pigskin and arranged in order; while Edwinson marked with delight the rows devoted to the classics, for he was a devoted scholar, although so pathetically second class. Smith let them busy themselves with inspection while he prepared an excellent coffee: soon they drank it, not unaccompanied by seductive liqueurs. Then pipes were lighted with English tobacco, glasses filled with Scotch whisky, and there sank into armchairs worthy of the noblest university traditions, two happy middle-aged schoolmasters, clothed in drab and a little beside themselves; and then it was that Harold stood before them with uplifted glass and swore in Italian, German, and English, that they should drink the health of their glorious profession, and drain their glasses to the Education of Youth.

CHAPTER II

THE AIM OF EDUCATION

SMITH roused no enthusiasm by proposing this toast. Hofman started and groaned, and Edwinson remarked sadly that he wanted to forget that dire, unspeakable thing.

SMITH. Is it possible that you hate your work, and that you are sincere in expressing your unhappiness? One would think there could be nothing more delightful than training the young and watching the subtle dawn of intelligence.

EDWINSON. Our work has its compensations, my dear Smith. Yet I cannot conceive of any vocation more disheartening, toilsome, and unpleasant.

SMITH. Yet perhaps you have not really any standard of comparison. What evidence have you that members of other professions are more cheerful than schoolmasters?

EDWINSON. I think I have some evidence. I have often been in the City, and observed narrowly the faces of the business men who pour out of the tube terminus. Anxious those faces often are, pale, feverish, elated with success, dejected with impending ruin; yet none of them were languid, none bored. Now you know, perhaps, that there is a special service held for schoolmasters and members of the Teachers' Union once a year in the chapel of some great public school.[1] I once attended such a service. There, in a narrow space, were collected some two hundred head and assistant masters. A more tragic sight I have never seen. It may be that the sermon, preached by a young Anglican of great eminence, had affected me strangely: but I know that when I left the chapel I nearly wept. Thank God one does not often see a congregation of schoolmasters. Those withered trees are usually surrounded by the fair and delectable shrubs of youth: they look ill in a forest by themselves. Usually we see the usher's unromantic figure graced by the boys who flock around him; and to them he is so familiar and trite a thing that they pay no heed to his sagging trousers and rusty coat, to his surly manners and unkempt hair, to his unchanging cravat and rectangular boots. But when I saw that unearthly congregation of men who had failed, whose lips were hard, and their faces drawn and sallow, when I remarked the imbecile athletes who taught football, the puny scientists who expounded the dark mystery of nature, the blighted and sapless scholars who taught Plato and Catullus by the page and hour, the little wry-bodied men in spectacles who trained their pupils in "King Lear" for the Cambridge Locals, I shuddered and felt faint; for I remembered that I, too, was one of these: I, too, was rusty—I effete—I growing old.

---

[1] Here Hofman snorted.

SMITH. You are convincing as to the fact, yet you hardly suggest a reason. Why is it, do you think, that teachers are such sad and bitter men?

EDWINSON. It is a little difficult to explain. Perhaps it is because we don't know——

HOFMAN. [*Interrupting violently.*] That's it. We do not know. We don't know where we are going to. We have no idea what sort of man we want to make, and while we have no definite aim we are beset by a million irritations from faddists and quacks. "Bring up boys and girls together," say some; "the school will then be a paradise." "Never teach a child what it doesn't want to know," says the benign paidophilist. God, I would like to teach him something he wouldn't like to know. "Science, grand, practical science!" says a crude person from the North; once I had faith in the crude person, before I taught grand, practical science. "Our old, beautiful traditions," say people like my friend here; "there is nothing wrong except the spread of scientific knowledge." "Modern tongues, not dead ones; something really useful to help the boys to good business positions." So clamour parents who do not realize that German clerks who know six languages to perfection may be purchased for about £160 a year. "English history, how splendid, how important!" says the blustering Member of Parliament, in a speech which would shame the school debating club, when he comes to give away our prizes. "English literature," cry the dames, "up to the death of Wordsworth, but including Tennyson, not omitting Beowulf if you want to understand Shakespeare." A pox on the fools; art, music, religion, and wood-carving—all have their votaries:

> Ce monde est plein de fous, et qui n'en veut pas voir
> Doit se tenir tout seul, ou casser son miroir.

EDWINSON. True, Hofman. Why, if I could get a paragraph into the " Daily Mail " suggesting that it is a disgraceful thing that our great public schools never teach Etruscan, which is not only the true foundation of any really thorough knowledge of Latin, but also a study most likely to foster mental ingenuity and deep thought, I should be styled " one of our most prominent educationalists " on the morrow. But since we are in such a vortex of new and absurd ideas, is there not some sense in keeping to the old lines? You have never understood, Hofman, and perhaps you never will, what is the true value and meaning of a classical education. Every year that this education continues to exist at all, it becomes more and more indispensable to any one who desires to understand history. We do not merely educate people to understand the world of Thucydides and Tacitus, Aeschylus and Virgil, but we educate them to understand Petrarch and Ariosto, Racine and Montesquieu, Pitt and Johnson and Pope, Milton, Landor, Shelley, Arnold, Browning, Tennyson, and Swinburne—for we have hardly had a great poet who was not a good classical scholar——

HOFMAN. Except Shakespeare!

EDWINSON. Even that is doubtful. To know the story of literature, of law, of science, and philosophy, you must study the classics; while a true and just use and knowledge of the subtleties of words may be inborn in a genius, but is the natural outcome of a scholar's training.

I readily admit that certain changes ought to take place from within. Wilamowitz-Moellendorf has made what I consider to be a quite admirable suggestion. He says in effect that we ought to read all Greek literature, and not confine ourselves to a little cluster of classical writers. He suggests that we should read Greek written as late as the tenth century A.D., and, indeed, the Byzantines are neither so uninteresting nor so incapable as is generally believed. With regard to the Latin tongue, I myself would rejoice to see the more suitable passages of Petronius, Apuleius, and the elegiacs of that dainty poet of the decline, Ausonius, included in the regular course. For I am a person of liberal ideas, though Hofman will credit me with none. I think, too, that one ought to get on much faster with the books one reads, and not spend a whole term droning through a book of Virgil at thirty lines a day. I believe that boys should be allowed to use translations: they are given plenty of Unseens on which to exert their minds, and I consider, though this is rather heresy, that only the most intelligent boys should be worried with Latin and Greek composition. We may teach our young Swinburnes or Jebbs to write Greek and Latin verses: I am not very much in favour of compelling the ordinary boy to undergo so severe a training.

You see, the grand old classics are waking up,

Hofman.   During the last few years the scientific
treatment of art and archaeology has made tremendous strides; while the study of folk-lore and comparative mythology is revolutionizing our ideas upon
Roman and Greek religion. Our comprehension of
the classics has advanced more between the year 1880
and the present time, than between the years 1600
and 1880. This is literally true. Then we still
find and always shall in the calm logic of Latin
grammar——

HOFMAN. [*Furiously.*] O Death! Do you dare to
insinuate that any one was ever taught to think about
the universe by learning perfects and supines, or those
eccentrics in—$\mu\iota$? Do you really think you are
going to ennoble and modernize the classics by skip-
ping through half a dozen wretched bastard Greek
romances written by a worthless people in a worthless
period, or by entertaining the lads with the cheerful
heresies of the early Christian Fathers? Do you say
keep the old system? Look at the result of your time-
honoured plan. One scholar (that is to say, one
naturally intelligent person whose intelligence you
have perverted to a useless end) to a hundred wastrels
(that is to say, a hundred ordinary young men whose
brains you have fuddled for ever). And your one
scholar, I grant you, may be a fine man—but wherein
lies his salvation? In being something more than a
scholar—in his self-education; in the music, art, or
poetry he loves, in his appreciation of the passions
and desires that sway the actual world. Can he even
be a fine scholar if he comprehends not these things?

Is a man who votes Tory because he is a don fit to understand Tacitus, or a man who has never travelled over the earth fit to enjoy the "Odyssey?" Shall we give Catullus to a passionless pedant, Ovid to a man who has never known Love's kiss? Even I, who have only read the classics in translations, have a better opinion of them than that.

I don't want to substitute science as being in any way a real or complete training for the young. My humble task is to teach the boys a few facts about the real world which may help them to earn their living, and I hate all rainbow theories of education. Teach a boy, I say, to read and write, and add up sums; then teach him his trade, and if you want a wider and a nobler upbringing for him, turn him loose into a good library for so many hours a day, and let him learn what he likes.

EDWINSON. [*Peevishly.*] Scholars can earn their living sometimes, and a fact in Latin grammar is as much a fact as a fact in physics.

SMITH. Come, brother Edwinson, I don't think you really mean that. You are arguing in a vicious circle if you maintain that a classical education is a practical one because your pupils may subsequently become classical teachers. You know of the tribe which existed by taking in each other's washing. You are well enough aware that the moment the dead languages cease to be required in State or University examinations which lead to emolument, the whole fabric of classical education instantly disappears; and the scholars who now secure for themselves snug and comfortable berths, would then be wandering up and down the land like disembodied spirits. A few might still be needed for museums and libraries, or to teach the sons of some old-fashioned American millionaire; but the rest would die of hunger or take to breaking stones.

Now I gather that you are, both of you—even Edwinson—rather disappointed in our English middle-class education. Do you then think that nothing could be done to reform our public schools?

HOFMAN. I think they are in such a state that reform is impossible, and that they ought to be utterly destroyed for ever. There is better work done in the dirtiest board school or technical training college in a day than we do in a week, and the public school is really such a loathsome place—

SMITH. You seem to be quite bitter about it, Hofman. In what way do you mean that a public school is loathsome?

HOFMAN. Why, were you never at one of those great institutions which make England what it is, and have made Balham and Bethnal Green what they are? Have you never witnessed the weary conflict between plodding dull ushers and stolid boys? Are you unaware of our finely organized system of compulsory cricket and compulsory vice? From the first of these evils a boy can only escape by being consumptive, from the second only by becoming a moral prig. Do you not know how the monotonous hours are only varied by epidemics, whether of chicken-pox, religion, silkworm-keeping, or Sandow exercises? Do you not know the hell that awaits all boys who think for themselves, who have any moral courage, who dare to look beyond the horizon of the damned routine, who shirk games, or who shirk looking at games?

SMITH. What you say has its truth. But to me it appears still worse that after this public-school life a boy should pass on to Oxford and Cambridge, where instead of entering on a new life he will merely continue in his former ways. If it meant influence to be a good cricketer at school, why so it does in college; if chapel was compulsory at school, so it is in college; if independence meant unpopularity at school, so it does in most colleges. No new society arises to entertain the mind, no women enable him to understand the proportion of things in this world ; no freedom of town life, no rousing interest in art or politics, will ever encroach on the monotony of a protracted schoolboy existence, wherein smoking, drinking, and cards are only occasionally restrained by authority.

EDWINSON. I am surprised that Hofman should thus depreciate school life, and that you, sir, should be so dissatisfied with the university. Consider how ninety-nine out of a hundred boys love their school, how they revel in school life, how they weep to leave it, and how they love to return and visit their old friends and masters. As for college—my days at Oxford were the only good days of my life, even though I never played cricket and football.

SMITH. Do you not consider what a terrible imputation it is against a school, if even the hundredth boy (unless he be a confirmed hypochondriac) be not happy? If you feed boys well, let them play with each other, and give them a reasonable amount of liberty, it is very hard to make them miserable. And in the generous days of youth who would not be sentimental about leaving friends and associations? But what Hofman says is that the best boys are the most unhappy—and I believe that, except possibly at Eton and Winchester, this is literally what happens. The new raw athletic mushroom public school is not a very pleasant place.

EDWINSON. But surely the Spartan element in our great schools is very fine. To rough it a little makes a boy independent and manly. A little bumping about— (Here Edwinson stopped, having caught an unpleasantly hostile expression in the eye of Harold Smith). Of course, all that is a little trite (he added lamely).

SMITH. Yes, Edwinson, that 's just it. A little bumping about will soon cure a boy of holding any ideas that displease his fellows, a little ridicule will soon cure Jones minor of reading Gibbon when he ought to be out in the rain watching the house hockey match, a really hard thrashing will soon dispel young Robinson's religious doubts. Oh, yes, we will embitter the seven years of life which should be the happiest, so as to give a boy more grit and pluck in after years. It seems we run a risk, Edwinson, and draw our bow at a venture. Does the nervous, high-strung youth become a thick-skinned Briton at the end of our Spartan training? I have not observed it: heresy of heresies, I do not really desire it. But I do very much fear that a boy of original mind may become permanently embittered and peevish under our present system and never acquire that strength and cheerfulness which underlies true genius. Our Spartan ideal is productive of minor poets, of most unmanly people who, claiming sanity and reserve, are ashamed instead of proud of what they think or feel or know; and I am so eccentric as not to be entirely pleased with that other notable product of our Lacedaemonian tendencies—the hulking and vain-glorious captain of the school eleven, whom I picture from memory standing crop in hand surrounded by his toadies and parasites, the terror and admiration of the young. Spartan system—why, the fellow has never been kicked since his very first term, when he made such a fine score in the Junior House match. Edwin-son, if the boys in your school are not happy, burn it down.

But there is a yet further question. Have you done your best for their happiness in the days of manhood, O pedagogue? For with that you are most intimately concerned.

HOFMAN. Have you then revealed your secret, Smith? Is that your ideal education which produces the happy man?

SMITH. Negatively, yes. That sounds cryptic; but I mean that whatever else we may strive after we fail if we do not help our pupils to be happy. In an uncertain world I take this as a postulate. But tell me, Hofman, since happiness is after all as difficult a word to explain precisely as goodness, the type of the man that you would desire to produce with the aid of education.

HOFMAN. [*With animation shining through his spectacles.*] I think education can do little to produce the type of man I want. I look for a man of power, an Overman, if you are not weary of the word. At any rate a man unflinchingly honest in his thoughts, and in the expression of his thoughts, unswayed by prejudice and convention, natural and strong in his desires and passions. A man who can pierce the riddle of this rather aimless existence and lead mankind to new triumphs and new glory.

SMITH. And you, Edwinson, perhaps do not entirely participate in Hofman's ideal?

EDWINSON. Indeed, no; he has expressed himself innocently enough, but I know he wants to turn all the nicest people into labour leaders. I confess I prefer the gentleman, if he will forgive me using a word he hates. I believe we have a duty to intimate society as well as to the State; and I believe that people with charming manners make life much more tolerable for their friends than unpleasant socialistic people.

HOFMAN. That is to say, gentlemen please other gentlemen.

EDWINSON. It is more than that. I have known many a boy whose head was perfectly empty, yet who had such a way with him that everybody liked him from the head master to the boot-black. But—be quiet, Hofman!—far be it from me to suggest that it is the business of a school to produce gentlemen. In a school to which gentlemen are sent the aim must be first that the blatancy of vulgarians should be toned down by association with boys of a more refined nature; secondly to produce in those who are gentlemen by birth a refinement, not only of manner and deportment, but also of language, taste, and thought —to produce not mere gentlemen, but that type of great gentleman whom we call a gentleman and a scholar.

SMITH. [*After a pause.*] Truth is dull, and I fear all I have to say is that both these ideals are excellent, and that they should and can be easily combined. But forgive me for remarking that they are ideals of admiration and not of thought. Both of you really want to produce men who shall be like yourselves.

HOFMAN. Or rather like our ideal selves. The men we might have been had we been blessed with opportunity.

SMITH. Well, then, you want to produce, perhaps, persons whom you would like to have as friends. But shall we not consider whether it would be possible to establish our discussion on a surer basis, and try to discover, not perhaps what the ideal man is, but at least what our ideal of a man is? We can at all events eliminate the elements which displease one or other of us. And if we do come to some more or less definite agreement on the subject, we shall hope that there may be many other sensible people in the wide world who would concur with our conclusions if they were here with us to-night.

We have already laid down one postulate, that we do not want to train our people to be miserable. We will lay down another, that we are not going to train our boys as candidates for any one of the various official paradises occupied by members of the rival sects. Is then the ideal of happiness enough? For if any one were to object that to train people to be happy would be to train them to be unpleasant, selfish, useless, and ignorant, we should reply that their notions of pleasure are ridiculous and limited. Happiness then——

EDWINSON. But surely you admire the noble ideas and fine morality, the devotion to work and duty, which have stamped the best men in the human race? And surely you do not believe that good men have acted merely because they would be happier in doing good? Even if such were really the case, it would be too horrible to believe, even as it is too horrible to believe that death is the end of all things, or that this universe has no aim.

HOFMAN. As usual, Edwinson, you take up that miserable Peer Gynt attitude: "Let us think of the things that are pleasant, and forget those that hurt" —and you send our pupils, as he sent his mother, headlong through the gate of death with ancient folk-tales and sweet, lying harmonies in their ears. What, do you yearn, O sentimental idealist, to set up the dusty old virtues on their feet again, and to clap on the statue of Truth the shabby rags of dying religions and the enormous fig-leaf of respectability? Let us make men who can realize themselves; for I weary of your heroes of the drawing-room and the popular stage; I am sick of the cant of devotion to one's duty, one's country, and one's only girl.

SMITH. But do you think that happiness will come from this self-realization of yours?

HOFMAN. What matter? We want men of power. The world is getting sick and rotten. We want some men who are free and brave. Where are the heroes who trampled us down in the gorgeous youth of the world?

SMITH. Your views do not differ materially from those of Edwinson, you know.

Hofman had for some moments been pacing the room in his excitement, and he now brought himself up to within a foot of the table on which Smith is sitting, and shouted " What? "

SMITH. Don't realize your voice like that, Hofman, or I shall fall off the table. My point is this. Both of you approve of virtue. But while Edwinson considers many qualities to be virtues, you only approve of Strength and Truthfulness, and I think your Overman will have to give up many things that mortals enjoy, such as Friendship and Love.

HOFMAN. But a man may be realizing himself in friendship and love.

SMITH. Not if self-realization means anything at all. I can understand how a man in pursuit of the ideals of power and self-realization may consider it advisable to understand his fellow-men and converse with them, but it is an obvious truth that friendship, love, and affection are bound to imply a subordination of oneself to others. Moreover, if life in a civilized state is to be tolerable, it entails considerable suppression of the natural man. But perhaps you would say that we realize ourselves by fitting ourselves to circumstances. I confess the term " self-realization" seems to me to be a little vague.

At all events, neither of you, I fear, seem to take kindly to my notion of educating people so that they may be happy. Now, Edwinson, what people would you consider to be most happy?

Edwinson rose slowly and went to the window. Below, on the opposite side of the street, a little crowd was waiting patiently and cheerfully for the doors of a cinematograph show to open. He pointed to the young workmen thronging down there with their wives on their arms and children dangling at their coats, and said:

EDWINSON. Those people, if they have good health and no aspirations, are probably as happy as any one in the world. Prosperous City men verging on middle age are, I expect, quite happy also. It is reserved for the sensitive men, for those whose fibre is weakened by learning and culture, to feel most deeply the misery of the world. It is education that makes a Leopardi bitter or drives a Baudelaire mad.

SMITH. To look at you and hear you speak, Edwinson, I should hardly believe that you had led a happy life. Yet do you really wish that your lot had been different? Do you yearn for the life of those poor men below? Would you really be content to plough fields or push barrows?

EDWINSON. No. Although in moments of depression I yearn for the happy, thoughtless existence of the ignorant, I would not really abandon my little knowledge; it is too precious to me, and I would not barter it against animal happiness. In knowledge, as in civilization, the further we advance the greater are our joys, the deeper our sorrows; but we cannot retreat.

SMITH. I am glad to hear you say so. Your words will help me to explain the type I desire to form, and they give me some hope that you will not hopelessly dissent from the views I am now going to express.

EDWINSON. Now let all profane tongues be silent, and let us hear and dispute the description of an ideal man.

SMITH. First, I admit that the term happy man embraces but little of our idea of a good man, of the men whom we would admire and love to own as a friend. Yet happiness (I would remark in passing), even of the lowest type, is something of a social virtue: it is pervasive and infectious, and therefore in a certain sense altruistic. I think we should most of us take more delight in the friendship of Rabelais than in that of Leopardi or Baudelaire—although, by the way, it was not only sensibility and intelligence but also incessant ill-health that made those two great men unhappy. Granted that we want our pupils to be cheerful, we must fit them for their station in life: we must train their physical health with the greatest care, and we must enable them to perform

the ordinary social duties of their station and to earn
a comfortable livelihood.

And yet we know well that some of the boys whom
we are going to teach will not be contented with this,
even while they are young. Man entertains fantastic,
inexplicable desires after things profitless—after truth,
knowledge, and beauty viewed as ends in themselves.
Some even yearn for absolute Chastity or absolute
Holiness. These latter two desires are spiritual, not
mental; exceptional, not rational; and since it has so
often been observed that holy men have an antipathy
to the use of human reason, we cannot undertake to
train our boys in holiness—for our business is with
thought. To my mind a passion for beautiful things
is the possession of the wise and thoughtful; or at
least is only of value to the intelligent: I cannot now
argue this philosophy, I can only appeal to the vivid
and trained understanding of those men who have
loved the beautiful. Therefore, since our concern is
with mental aspirations, and since we must accept it
as a fact that men do long to understand the problems
of reason, to master the details of science, and to
appreciate beautiful things, and that we in fact admire and love the men who hold these strange desires
—we will lay down that a fuller education be given
in our schools to those who are fitted to receive it.
Our scholars who taste of the bitter-sweet fruit of this
tree of knowledge will be made both more happy and
more miserable. But observe, though we educate
them for the sake of that greater happiness to which
they will attain, yet we are not deluded into thinking

that the young man who is athirst for knowledge is athirst for happiness. Some happiness it may give him, but that is only by the way. Foolish and irritating are those who contend, " This man gives his money to the poor because it is his form of pleasure; my form of pleasure is to expend it on the racecourse: there is no moral difference between us!" If a man prefers to be generous, it is just this preference of his that makes us call him a good man: and we call him good not really in accordance with any fixed moral code, but from the nature of ourselves, which is to admire strong will, strong intellect, and strong love in our fellow-men.

HOFMAN. But supposing some people, as some do, admire Charles Peace the burglar extremely, and others think him an outrageous scoundrel?

SMITH. The difference here and in all cases is not one of the natural faculties of admiration, but of analysis of the case. One man admires in Peace his strength of will, his intellect, his energy; another detests his lack of love. To admire energy and to hate cruelty is universal. But are you now agreed that the formation of some such type as I have described is a worthy aim for education?

EDWINSON. You have made clear to me ideas that I felt for myself, but could not clearly define or express.

HOFMAN. And I am most marvellously persuaded.

After this the conversation became much less serious, and I grieve to state that Hofman began to feel a strange inclination to dance and sing. So they wore him out by taking him a very long walk round the city; and then Smith left them, but not without a solemn promise that he would meet them early on the morrow.

III

HAROLD SMITH met the two schoolmasters, as arranged, comparatively early the next morning at a café. He found them ruefully consuming thin coffee and thick rolls, and pining for the fleshpots and teapots of England. He laughed at their dejected countenances and gleefully produced from his pocket a fine pot of jam, which he good-naturedly shared with the forlorn travellers. The little party became most amicable, and as it was a fine fresh morning they resolved to make an expedition into the country. Their plans grew gradually more extensive and ambitious, till finally they decided to quit Bologna with no baggage but knapsacks, and to return thither only after some days of pedestrian exploration beyond the Apennines. They therefore took the train for a few miles so as to get on the foot of the mountains, alighted at an insignificant station on the line to Florence, and walked along the pass as far as Bagni di Poretta, where they took rooms for the night, and dined handsomely. Over coffee and cigars Hofman became expansive, and glowed as ruddy as his beard with delight. "What a day, what a walk!" he cried; "I feel quite young again. Smith, you're making new men of us poor schoolmasters. I wish you didn't walk at such a pace, though. I should never have thought you were such an athlete to look at you."

EDWINSON. It has been a fine excursion indeed. Enough exercise to make us comfortably tired, not enough to exhaust or take away the appetite. I'm feeling wide awake; if you people are willing, let's go on talking about education.

HOFMAN. I should love to if it doesn't bore Smith, for I want to hear more wisdom from the mouth of that wise young man. It strikes me as odd, you know, Edwinson, that at school we never said a word, either to each other or to any one else, about the general principles and aims of education. We used, of course, to get quite excited about new or peculiar methods of pumping in knowledge, but we never really considered where—well, where——

SMITH. Where you were going to drive to when you'd got the tyres tight—if I may adopt your own cheery metaphorical style, Hofman?

EDWINSON. And whither shall we drive to-night, O charioteer?

SMITH. Straight on. In the distance our road may be obscure, but we shall have no immediate difficulty in finding our way. For we are at least certain of to-night's destination. Physical training we must discuss; and here all sane men are with us in our efforts to discover how to preserve, maintain, and encourage health in our pupils. However, since we are not doctors, we must, I fear, confine ourselves to generalities.

Now health, I think, should be, as they say, not

merely a harmony after the Platonic style, but positive and exuberant.

EDWINSON. Won't that tend to some rather depressing forms of heartiness? I don't like people who slap one on the back and poke one in the ribs.

SMITH. I don't much mind the type, especially among boys. It only means that the intellect of your hearty man is not as well trained as his body, or that the aggressor has not enough natural outlet for the exercise of his vivid animal strength. Or it may be that he has not learnt manners. And the hearty only offend those who are feeling weak and depressed. In this mountain air, my dear Edwinson, you are getting quite hearty yourself, and I confidently expect to see you playing leap-frog with Hofman to-morrow all the way down to Pistoia.

HOFMAN. [*With an air of raising the tone of the conversation and suggesting a good theory for contentious debate.*] All schools should be on heights. It is curious that altitude should not only invigorate the body but elevate the mind.

SMITH. Height is not very necessary, Hofman, and has become a mania with some people, who seem to imagine that the Spartans exposed their babies on the peak of Taÿgetus in order to improve their health. Pure air is what a school needs, but this pure air is of little use unless we breathe it all night long. All our boys will sleep in the open air, with just enough shelter to protect them from rain. Colds will be a thing of the past; the " general health " of the school will improve beyond belief; and not a school in England has the courage to do it.

Let us now build our beautiful school on the hills of imagination, and let us build it on the south coast of England. For I have a great faith in sunshine and sea.

HOFMAN. Down in Hampshire there is a little village beside a great warm bay which I loved best of all places when I was a boy. Eastward a long, wonderful spit of hard and shell-strewn sand divides the bay from the all-but-lake of a harbour; westward rise white cliffs through which the tunnelling agents of the world have delved unknown and secret caves, or carved striding hollow rocks such as Turner drew in his Polyphemus, islanded out to sea. On land you have a little level strip near the sea for playing fields and a little shaven down on which to build the school in all its pride; and near by are moors, yellow in spring and red in autumn, to keep our fancies young.

SMITH. I know your unnamed bay and its gentle scenery. Let us build there the school of our dreams, and one day perhaps we will build on that shaven down a school in substance and reality. For dreams have been realized before now, my friend, even schoolmasters' dreams. Or have you never heard of La Giocosa and the fair name of that great humanist, Vittorino da Feltre, and how he taught his Mantuans the rhythm of body and mind, and was loved by them as few schoolmasters have been loved before or since those bright Renaissance days? Yet even in our imaginations and schemes let us be honourably fearless, bold, and practical, and imagine not, like the bad poet, a golden and misty dream, but like the good poet, a strong and stirring reality. And since we must construct the shape before we infuse the spirit, let us first consider our portals and windows. In what style shall our architect build?

EDWINSON. Shall he build in splendid Gothic, to match our old schools and cathedrals of England?

SMITH. I hope not. Revived Gothic has produced no single good building in England, nor are ill-lighted vaults suitable for a school. We will have nothing to do with renewals of old styles; we will not build after the Greek fashion, or the Graeco-Roman, or the Full Roman, or Byzantine, or the Moorish, or the Perpendicular, or the Jacobean, or the Gothic, or the Ruskin-Gothic. Our style must be as new as our school. We will not oblige ourselves to build in stone because stone is symbolic, nor in brick because brick is so lowly and Hebraic. We shall build for comfort and utility, and obtain our beauty not from the added ornamentation of an antique style, but from the principles of symmetry and design. Indeed, I imagine we shall build our school after the American manner, with iron and reinforced concrete. Of all methods of construction this is the strongest, for the San Francisco earthquake itself could not shake down the tallest and slimmest buildings wrought of this material. Therefore, we shall build our school with straight and simple harmonious lines; and in so doing we may perhaps be advancing into a new architectural style, some day to be reckoned great and in its turn worthy of imitation.

EDWINSON. I feel it would be very horrible to copy anything American, and the idea of this shed arrangement of yours chills me. Won't it look rather like a powder magazine, with its great, bare, white walls?

SMITH. Who said we were going to have bare white walls? The delight and joy of my building will be in fresco and statuary, not in pointed windows, mullions, and leaded panes. On the outside the school shall be a blaze of colours—and if frescoes fade, even in the South of England, so much the better for the artists of future generations, who will have to come and paint us new ones. Why, we will get the greatest pointillist artist alive to do our frescoes, for those sunlight effects of his that can never be seen at a proper distance in galleries will be grand in the open air. But it would be out of place to consider these details now: we must attack the problem of health, and waiving romance, consider our building from the sanitary point of view. That simplicity of construction which we have chosen will surely go far to solve the problems of hygiene. Easy ventilation, no corners for dirt, central heating, mechanical dust extraction, desks arranged so that the light comes over the boys' left shoulders, electric light with shaded globes, no carpets, mouldings, fire-grates, but a few easily beaten mats and running water in every bedroom, these things will be obvious necessities to so modern an architect as ours, and we need say no more about them. We must have also a sanatorium under the direct management of a resident doctor. Strange it is, though, that any school which has the impertinence to ask over a hundred pounds a year for training and keeping boys as boarders should be destitute of these advantages.

HOFMAN. But we have not yet entered directly into the subject of physical training. Is there really any necessity to do so? I should have thought that we overdo it, if anything, in our English schools.

SMITH. Our system of games—and, considering all things, what a splendid system it is!—is quite unique. Do not laugh at me, Hofman, I mean something more than a platitude. Nowhere abroad, unless we count America, can it be paralleled. On the whole, it makes for the happiness of boys. Compare the merry and confident aspect of our English youth with the miserable, pinched, prematurely earnest appearance of continental children. Think of the lives of German schoolboys, embittered by the deadly gymnastics, the huge classes, the incessant cram, the perpetual and ruinous horror of the final examination. Think of the ghastly statistics of child suicide in Prussia. Is it not this appalling system that is making the modern German so different a man from the old—is making him the great brutalizing force of the world? How glorious is England in comparison! Perhaps, indeed, our discussion is futile: did all public schools give such a mental education as the most intelligent boys receive at Winchester and Eton, it would seem rash and Utopian to expect still finer things of English education, for the physical part of it is so invariably excellent. But still, if there be little room for improvement, so much the easier to fill up the space. And after all, our system of games and sports has become very perverted.

My great objection is that we have so little variety in our games. Cricket, for instance, is usually the sole diversion of a boy's summer term, except in the case of the three or four schools which practise rowing. There is no better game (we have heard this perhaps a little too often) for encouraging adroitness of hand and quickness of eye; but it is of no more use in the formation of bodily vigour and beauty than any other outdoor, not sedentary, occupation. Now cricket is a pastime which only the proficient can possibly enjoy, that is to say, it is a game fit for about half the school. What happens to the other boys in the long summer afternoons? Are they allowed to take such exercises as they please, to walk, bicycle, or play tennis? Very rarely. Is there any school in Britain where boys are taught those two superb, manly, and most British exercises—the riding of a horse and the sailing of a ship? Is then the only reasonable alternative enforced? Are the boys who dislike cricket and incompetent at it taught the game with special care, and helped to take their part by diligent individual instruction, like boys who are backward in their work? No, not anywhere in the kingdom. What happens in most large schools is that there are special games made up of athletic dullards, who are set three times a week or more to play out amongst each other the weariest, the most melancholy of farces, captained by some unathletic, ineffectual classical scholar. For five hours the diverting sport continues, interrupted by a roll call, which ensures that no reprobate shall have shirked this noble duty for a little aimless wandering among woods and hills. Only too well do these incompetent and despicable boys (none of them, I am sure, of the stuff which has made England what she is) know the emptiness of waiting, the interminable dullness of fielding, the too brief joy of batting. Thus trained to perceive the inner charm of cricket, what a welcome change, what an instructive education, to spend from time to time a whole sun-bright afternoon watching, by compulsion, school matches.

The trouble in England is that we have never taken games seriously enough. We look upon them as a spectacle or show on a level with the music hall and the variety entertainment. How else could we endure the existence of professionals? In true sport no professionalism could ever be admitted; but as the thing is a show, why, the professionals make it a better show. Let us have professionals to instruct our boys and to roll the pitch; for what other reason an intelligent English sportsman should desire their existence I cannot tell.

If we really consider the matter, we have never treated athletics as a vital part of our national physical training. We are always intent upon the show games. We forget that it is infinitely more important that boys should enjoy themselves in some healthy way really suited to their natures, than that they should become adepts in cricket or football.

HOFMAN. Cricket and similar games do, I suppose, train character, and there is a legend that they train boys in unselfishness, although I have not particularly remarked that school athletes are of a sweet, unselfish, retiring disposition. But I must say I do not consider cricket an ideal way of spending the afternoon, even for the proficient cricketers. It is played in the open air, but it is not part of the outdoor life as I understand it.

SMITH. What do you mean by the outdoor life?

HOFMAN. I suppose I am thinking of my favourite pupils who spend the afternoon with me exploring old quarries in the search of fossils, or grubbing in ditches for rare plants, or tracking birds and beasts with infinite stealth to their lairs, not to destroy but to observe. I look at them, tired, healthy, happy, and voracious, returning from a long tramp. Would that afternoon have been better spent even in the most brilliant cricket? The fact is, it's so much less trouble to make all boys play one game and stick to one occupation. I rather think it's a neglect of duty on the part of their teachers.

SMITH. You are right as far as you go, Hofman. I think it is clear that we must have more variety in our games and occupations. Even pure athletics, such as running and swimming, are rather neglected; there are a thousand other games little played in schools, yet not contemptible and not unsuitable for boys—fives, golf, tennis, lacrosse. What boy even learns to punt, or is seriously taught to drive a motor? Edwinson will doubtlessly tell us that football and especially cricket are very beautiful, picturesque games, very traditional and fine. But we are concerned with English physique, which is more important than English cricket, and to improve this physique we must subject our weak or ill-formed boys to special training. Men who play cricket well may be round-shouldered, men who row well may over-develop themselves on one side, and, according to a well-substantiated legend, if they row too well they die young. Gymnasts tend to assimilate to the Eugene Sandow type, to become of dwarfed and monstrous appearance, with exaggerated muscles standing out in knobs all over their bodies. Rather, then, my dear Edwinson, we will revert to the MHΔEN AΓAN of your beloved Greeks; we will be mindful of the types of Polycleitus. To do this we must give a special, not a general, gymnastic training; we must take our athletics more seriously, and spend more trouble over them. We will not permit boys to stand in platoons and swing bars up and down; we will not be delighted to watch them promiscuously scrambling over the horse and up the ladder; we will not let them grow into short and hideous gymnasts, but we will, with the aid of medical wisdom and specialized gymnastics, cure round shoulders, narrow chests, and spindle arms; and I think we shall be rewarded for our pains.

HOFMAN. Would you not teach them also something about the laws of health and the structure of the human body?

SMITH. The older boys and those who are going to be doctors or artists may learn all they like. How to bandage a wound, how to save life, what to take for a cold every one should know. But we must be very careful, or we may give them that little knowledge which is so dangerous; they will either not say when they are ill and try to cure themselves, or whenever they have a pain in the back they will come trembling to us and announce that they have Bright's disease.

HOFMAN. Then about hours of work, holidays and so forth, are you contented with the present-day system? I think it is an important question.

SMITH. There seems little to suggest. There should be far less preparation of work in evenings, far more direct plunging into a new subject in class. There should never be any work before breakfast at all, but boys might get up earlier than they usually do—at about 6.30 in summer, bathe, and have breakfast at once; while in winter they need not rise till about eight o'clock. The youngest boys, however, ought not to get up as early as suggested in summer, or their day will be too long. There should be two half-holidays a week in the winter terms with a short and interesting hour's work in the late afternoon, but three full half-holidays a week in summer; and every opportunity should be given to boys for spending their Sundays in excursions over the country-side, for the attendant evils of these excursions—the irate farmer whose horse has been ridden round a field, the boy with the catapult, the boy who goes into a public house to be grand and drinks a mug of beer, and the boy who surreptitiously buys Black Dog cigarettes—are not very terrible after all, and the attendant advantages are too great to be missed.

HOFMAN. We shall not, I hope, maintain discipline with the rod?

SMITH. We shall, Hofman. There is, I admit, a certain peril of the flagellant vices. But we must run so inconsiderable a risk for the sake of considerable advantages. At any rate we shall not lend ourselves to the vulgar opinion of those sentimentalists who consider it degrading to endure physical pain, and laying a practically obscene stress on the torments of physical discomfort, pathetically invite us to use moral suasion. Punishment is absolutely necessary in a large school. It must be proportionable to the offence, and the only two possible punishments that are so proportionable are detention and caning. In the hours of detention we should insist that a boy be occupied in some form of hard but profitable work; malicious penalties, such as the assignment of " lines," we shall esteem beneath us. Boys would usually themselves prefer to be dealt with quickly and summarily, and it is very possible we shall give them the choice of treatment when we can. Most head masters nowadays are extremely careful not to touch particularly delicate and nervous boys, and the days when floggings in school were a real and serious evil ceased with the death of that head master, often called great, who made his school famous as the place " where they flogged the boys so." When we punish boys we shall, I fear, have to lecture them a little; they must be aware of our displeasure, particularly if the offence is of a mean or underhand kind; they must be clearly shown that they have done the sort of thing the best boys do not do. On the other hand, if they are caught smoking, or arraigned for juvenile clamour, we will not weep over the enormity of the offence, but deal with it succinctly. I may be wrong in this; to tell you the truth, I consider the sentimentalist more poisonous than the flagellant.

EDWINSON. We have, perhaps, left the most difficult problem untouched.

SMITH. [*Cheerfully.*] Oh, the sex problem: there is no difficulty about that. Or if there is, it lies in the sentimental obtuseness of the public. Wells has settled the matter for ever by suggesting a book on the subject; and such a book every boy in the school shall possess. It must contain the exact truth without exaggerating dangers or threatening hell. It must clearly state that the popular prejudices are against certain things, without agreeing or disagreeing with those prejudices. It will clearly add that, for the school's sake, any immorality discovered will be severely and corporally punished. We can avoid in our open-air system as well as in any other those pernicious partitioned dormitories, which so obviously foster vice. We shall not expel boys; and we shall not, like the conventional head master, pretend to faint with horror when we discover others acting as we might perhaps with a little temptation have acted ourselves, had we ever been members of so monastic an establishment as a public school.

EDWINSON. The chapel is perhaps a help.

SMITH. Emotional purity in the young is to my mind an insidious form of indecency. It is laying too much stress on things. The normal boy troubles as little about the matter as possible: and he is perfectly and entirely right.

So saying, Smith seemed to think he had exhausted the question, for he changed the subject a little abruptly, and began to criticize the poetry of Browning.

IV

TECHNICAL TRAINING

THE three friends were at Pistoia.

They had arrived a little after noon, and had spent an hour or two already in observation, and were entranced that this little town should be a treasure-mine of beauty, and contain more fair and noble creations than three English counties. For in it are many large churches of white marble striped with black, fascinating the curious. And there is a pleasant Duomo and a noble baptistery. And a superb pulpit by him of Pisa, who first learnt from unearthed Greek marbles that even stone men may move and be divine. And very old curious reliefs by Gruamons and Adodat, who did not know this. And, above all, there is the finest work of the Della Robbias, that frieze on the Ospedale, where in bright-coloured relief are sweetly represented the seven Works of Mercy. Thus it was that, possessed by that peace and largeness of the spirit that comes to those who have lovingly contemplated works of beauty and structures of delight, they sat down in the evening in a little café in a side street and, just as the last rays of sunset were leaning across the plain to kiss the Apennines, earnestly re-opened their discussion.

HOFMAN. As far as I can remember what you said

at Bologna, we must now deal with technical training, that is, with instruction given in order to enable our boys to earn their livings. It seems we must either give a few general ideas or enter into a mass of detail and suggest what is necessary for each profession or trade.

EDWINSON. Trade? I presumed we were reforming the ordinary English public school. Are we going to reform board-school education as well?

SMITH. We cannot talk about a select school while we are considering ideals of education.

EDWINSON. But we cannot under any conceivable circumstances educate together our diplomats and our shoe-blacks.

SMITH. Which would be injured most if we did, I wonder: our diplomats or our shoe-blacks?

EDWINSON. It would only vulgarize our diplomats and make our shoe-blacks discontented.

SMITH. Then you consider that discontent in a shoe-black is not divine, and that the quality of a gentleman is skin deep? Never mind, Edwinson. You believe in aristocracy, and so do I. You hate vulgarity of manners; I dislike it also, but not as much as I dislike vulgarity of mind. If I do not hold your belief in the British aristocracy of to-day it is because I find that most of them, except those few who are actively engaged in State service, are both vacuous and vulgar. You may know them better than I do, but, as far as I can judge, their views on art and life are as vulgar as their taste in amusement and their attitudes in motor cars. Our philosophers and

artists find little of the encouragement from them
which they would have infallibly obtained two hundred years ago; they have been forced to take sides
with democracy. Some day, perhaps, our men of
sense and wisdom will form a party to themselves
and wrest the reins of government from demagogues
and quacks. But you know well enough that our
best and most venerable public schools contain numbers of boys whose grandfathers were, shall we say,
shoe-blacks, and that some of these boys are tolerable
and some the reverse, because some have minds and
some have not. It is education that refines and
mental quiescence that degrades. We will have no
deformed natures in our school; but we will teach all
who are capable of receiving instruction how to talk
pleasant English and to behave prettily. Phonetics
will help us. And any poor boy of mean birth who
shows himself worthy of the higher education shall
receive it. We will make a scheme to help them out
of the school funds, partly by giving scholarships,
partly by lending them money to be repaid when
they are in secure positions, earning a fair income. If
a duke's son, on the other hand, shows himself incapable of learning manners, he shall either learn the
trade for which he is fitted or leave us.

EDWINSON. I am afraid the dukes will not send
their sons to us.

SMITH. Then we will hope to have the sons of
north country artisans: the class has begun to think
independently and to delight in reading, and they are
the best class of men in England. But to return to

our technical training. Not only is it impossible to talk about separate trade details, but also impossible to build the small town which we would require if we were going to teach a number of trades. A boy will have to leave school early if he wants to specialize in book-binding or horse training. So we will talk first of all of those things which will be useful to all boys throughout life, and beginning at the beginning we must consider reading and writing. We must teach them spelling rationally and by derivation.

EDWINSON. But if they know no Latin?

SMITH. A boy can learn that *medius* means middle without spending years at Cicero and Horace. You can tell a boy that the word we pronounce fewsha is connected with the German for a fox, even if he hasn't read and could not read the second part of "Faust." And I don't much mind about spelling when all is said and done: it is matter of a special faculty of observation, and a man may be a splendid engineer and write "parallel" with an "l" too few. That boys ought to read beautifully is a fact so obvious that it has been universally forgotten: our young men are a tribe of mumblers. But it is about writing that I have very definite suggestions to make. I am convinced of the futility of copy-books, double-lined paper, and all other aids to calligraphy. I am persuaded that it is absurd to worry about the writing of a child of ten: I am also persuaded that it is very important to worry about the writing of a boy of fifteen. To teach beauty of writing is perhaps impossible; the beauty of a writing lies in its character, and nothing is more revolting than a copper-plate fist. But we can teach legibility, and even speed.

Then we should consider arithmetic. But, Hofman, you know more about that than I do.

HOFMAN. I think I can point out to you a serious mistake which modern educationalists make. They want little boys to be so intelligent. They yearn to show them the reason of things. They would like them to work out for themselves the theory of subtraction, and they revel in a horribly complicated system of shortened division. It is so much easier for a small boy to learn things by rule. Let the problems of numbers come when he has learnt his tables, and can add up money, and has mastered the fair twin systems of fractions.

SMITH. Yes, Hofman, and do you think we need worry them with any but the most important of our horrible weights and measures? Might we not keep hidden from them the mysteries of pecks, scruples, and bushels till they come actually to need them, and abolish discount sums, stock and share sums, compound interest sums till the days when they have more than fourpence a week to spend on speculation? Shall we not tire of papering rectangular rooms with square windows? But since we are going to have workshops they will be able to take a practical interest in many of these things. The measuring of the wood and the calculation of its price will not in our school be left to the carpenter, and the misfits of home-made cupboard doors will give them sound lessons in practical geometry.

EDWINSON. We have now mentioned reading, writing, and arithmetic. Will our hopelessly stupid people, our bricklayers and boot-blacks, need anything more?

SMITH. In the ideal state, as I conceive it, they would not. The government would ensure that these limited individuals should live in comfort and cleanliness, and be paid in proportion to the simplicity of their occupations. In an ideal country, if any of them in after years found his intellect developing, and began to read books in our free libraries, he could at any time take the State examination, and, by passing it, become entitled to a more profitable and less humdrum occupation.

HOFMAN. If schools like ours were established all over this ideal England, and if you were to give all boys a real chance, unskilled labour would become very dear.

SMITH. Then we shall have to invent more machines to take the place of unskilled labour, my dear Hofman. But we do not live in an ideal England, but in a country where the stupidest boys may be the heirs to fortunes, for all we know, and where they all will certainly be entitled to votes. Let us then consider what might be done under existing circumstances. I think our plan will be this. We will wait till the boys are fifteen years old, and then we will take those who are deriving no benefit from their more advanced classes which they attend, and put them in a class together, where we must endeavour to teach them, if we can, the elementary rules of argument, and even show them that they need not believe a thing because it is printed and published. We shall, perhaps, be able to do this by means of examples of vicious argument and *petitiones principii* culled from the daily papers. Also they ought to know a little of the inner working of political events during the last twenty years, and we will read to them the best stories of English history to make them proud of their country. Also, if we are cynical, we will teach them the doctrines of Carlyle to make them proud of their work. And if a Plato arises to turn political economy into something at once simple and profound, we will teach them that. We shall fail, perhaps, to make any impression on these unfortunates, but we shall not have been guilty of neglect.

HOFMAN. But the difficulty is that we cannot really divide our school up into sheep and goats, or wise and foolish, even by examination. We are going to have, in our school, boys of a hundred different grades of intelligence, a hundred different aptitudes.

SMITH. And we shall have to grade our instruction accordingly. Our guardians, our brilliant boys, our ΦΥΛΑΚΕΣ will learn everything they can. But obviously our doctors will have more of the instruction we give to our ΦΥΛΑΚΕΣ than our bakers or butchers. All that is a mere matter of detail.

HOFMAN. Ah, had you ever been a schoolmaster, Smith, you would not prattle so merrily about matters of detail. We have not yet said a word about the higher education: but look at the mess in which we are already involved. Boys who are going to be boot-blacks will be attending the bottom class in political economy; boys in the top class of political economy will be attending the lowest class in boot-blacking. It seems your rule is simply this, that we are going to teach everybody everything they can learn.

SMITH. Not such a bad ideal either, Hofman; but the picture you draw is perverse and unjust. However, I think it would be better to put a little order into the apparent chaos in this way. We are going to draw a sharp dividing line in our table of school hours. The morning will be spent entirely in teaching boys things that will help them to earn their money. The morning will be devoted to workshops, bookkeeping, shorthand, all work of any sort that is done with the object of passing examinations, not excluding that specialized training in writing Greek and Latin poetry, which enables a man to gain scholarships and earn his living as a don. Of course it will be hard to arrange, for boys may be going to earn money in a thousand different ways; but we have pointed out that very few of the more specialized sorts of technical training can be given in school. It comes to little more than saying that the ordinary school work done on the scientific or modern side of an up-to-date school day will be compressed into the morning, with the huge advantage that we are neither going to worry our scientist with Greek irregular verbs nor our architects with chemistry from the moment when the boy or his parents or we ourselves, judging from the boy's preferences and character, have decided

what profession he is to follow. Before the age of
fifteen, by which time he ought to have made up his
mind, a boy will be given his chance of working at
various studies and occupations to test his capacity or
preference.

The afternoon we shall employ in real education—
but Florence is the place where we will talk of that,
nor could I imagine a better scene for so high a
discussion.

EDWINSON. It is a pity we cannot connect Pistoia,
too, with our technical training, since Florence will
be so suitable, and we connected Bologna with the
inaugural discussion, and the mountain heights with
physical accomplishments.

SMITH. Well, Pistoia used to be a great manu-
facturing town in the old days. It was the birthplace
of pistols: hence its name.

HOFMAN. See " Baedeker "

V

THE GRECIANS, OR TRUE EDUCATION

THE melodious name of Florence calls up such delightful and extravagant memories that many wayfarers, who have the love of books and pictures in their souls, have been disappointed with the austere appearance of the city, with her narrow yet straight and gloomy streets, her huge rectangular palaces, her vast and unsatisfying cathedral. But if on a summer afternoon a man should ascend, as our friends ascended, the hill of Fiesole, he would see from that famous eminence the City of Flowers, wonderfully set among her gardens and villas, and he would appreciate that tremendous dome which rises high above the plain of Arno, like some fabled antique omphalos of the world, and he might cry, perverting to himself that gentle ballad of old:

> Where will you bury me? In Saint Mary of the Flowers.
> Wherewith will you cover me? With violets and roses.

They sat on the terrace of a little inn gazing at the prospect in the glorious light of afternoon, for they had already stretched forth their hands over the dainties, and eaten and drunk in abundance. It had been arranged that they should not discuss what Smith called true education, but that he should write down for them his thoughts on the subject in connected form. And this he had done.

"Do let us hear you read now, Harold," said Edwinson.

The young man took a sheaf of paper out of his pocket and quietly began.

"I require that those who listen to my words should hold one faith with me. They must believe with me in the value of human reason; they must love beautiful things and consider them important; they must be enthusiastic for their fellow-men. They must believe that it is possible to learn, and even that it is possible to teach. Otherwise my words will be vain and convey neither meaning nor persuasion.

"I have to realize that I have little new to say. I, like Plato, desire to create ΦΥΛΑΚΕΣ. If we really understand that golden book of the 'Republic,' such a type of the classic in its form, so strangely modern in its theory, so simple and so subtle, we shall perhaps think that no more need be said, and that by close following of its precepts we may be able to create ΦΥΛΑΚΕΣ in modern England. We must realize that in attacking poetry as a means of education, Plato is merely attacking, under a decent veil, the popular religion of which Homer was the Bible; we must be perpetually on the watch for Plato's quiet humour: and then the 'Republic' becomes for us in practical matters a wise and attractive guide. Yet we have to adapt Plato's theories to the modern world, and that is what I shall now attempt. Forgive me, then, if I become dull, prosaic, and detailed in my ardour for common sense. I have not prepared a surprise for you; I am not going to expound any startling or novel theory; I am not going to suggest a short cut to perfection; but I am going to trace out in detail a course of education which I hope will appeal to the thoughtful as possible, desirable, and sufficient.

"I must suppose, moreover, for my purposes, that the school which is to rise on that bright English bay of ours will somewhat partake of the nature of a university. I must have at least five years of a boy's intelligent life. For the education I intend to give to those who are fit to receive it (whom I intend henceforward to call Grecians, borrowing a delightful term from the traditions of Christ's Hospital), is very universal and very difficult. Keeping clear before me all the danger I run of turning my pupils into *dilettanti*, I am going to teach them to be as far as possible universal in their comprehension and admiration of the mysteries and beauties of life. Our Grecians, when they leave us, will have seen, as it were from a height suddenly, the whole world of knowledge stretching out in rich plains and untraversed seas.

"Let me at this point lay down very clearly who these Grecians of mine will be. I intend education to be given, in the complete form which I am going to describe, to those boys in the school who have the best and most refined intelligence. In an ideal state these boys would not have to earn their living: they would automatically become rulers of the State, or else be subsidized to live in leisure as artists or critics. In our actual England we can give this complete education only to the sons of the rich, and to those few boys which our school funds enable us to support, not only here, but afterwards. To give a boy this complete education, we must keep him till he is at least twenty-one. In England of the present day he would find himself at that age well prepared to take, after another year's special work, such an examination as that admitting to the Indian Civil Service. I mention this, because it may show that some parents might risk leaving their sons with us to receive a useless and fine education, and yet hope that boys so educated might subsequently earn their livings even in the existing state of society. But the whole virtue and beauty of true education must depend on its absolute isolation from the prying influence of the State or University. I do not mean by this that we shall object to examinations as such, but will have nothing to do with examinations which lead us out of our chosen path. Our only examinations will be the school examinations. By examining boys, and by no other method, shall we admit them to our select company; by examining we will assign to them their rank in the school. I have little patience with those who abuse examinations. An examiner may be stupid and set worthless papers; but provided the papers be well set, examination is the sole adequate test of a boy's capacity. For we have no sympathy with Cecil Rhodes, nor with the cheerful, popular, and chiefly ignorant crowds who come to Oxford under his fantastic testament: we do not like this democratic selection of the prize favourites: we pin our faith to a written and evident intellectual superiority. We mistrust the boy who is said to be 'very good at work really, but no use at exams.' Such a boy is either so morally deficient that he cannot rise to a crisis and concentrate his energy and ideas—and far be it from me to admit such a one to be a Grecian—or else it means that he is incapable of literary composition or self-expression; or else that his thoughts and facts are so confused that he cannot write them down. There is a great deal wrong with boys who fail at examinations. Furthermore, I believe in prizes; I refuse to expect the young, however intelligent they may be, and however delightful they may find their studies, to show that single-hearted devotion to work which we demand of the research scholar or the specialist.

"How, then, shall we select those boys who are to be given this most full education? Entirely from those who are most proficient in the afternoon work. What I am going to discuss now is the education that the highest form in the school will receive. Boys who arrive at this high standard will be, where possible, exempt from the technical training accorded to others: they will devote morning and afternoon to the culture of the mind. Now all boys in the school will be compelled to take part in this afternoon work, be they stupid or clever, old or young. The more intelligent they are, the more their profession will have to suit itself to their education. But we have not thought it worth while to do more than suggest by references here and there, what the afternoon education will mean in early years. And if I have confused the ideal and real at times, I think I may be excused, for it is in reality quite easy to perceive how far my ideal could be followed at the present day. But to make quite clear what I actually intend, I will trace the ordinary careers of Auberon, Arthur, Jack, Montague, Peter, and Tom.

"Auberon is the son of a rich nobleman who has every faith in a humane education. He does not require his boy to prepare for any examinations, as he can get a diplomatic or other post if the boy demands one. Auberon arrives at school between the ages of ten and twelve, knowing how to read, write, and add. As he is under no necessity of learning a trade, or fitting himself for a professional examination, he spends the morning hours attending lessons in the Latin and French languages, which are being given to those boys who have to take examinations in the subject. He shines in the afternoon classes; he has a passion for reading plays, and is never weary of observing pictures. In after years he soon passes the examination which admits him into our Grecians, and follows their course of education, which will shortly be described, staying with us to the age of twenty-one.

"Arthur is little less gifted by nature than Auberon, but his father cannot support him in after life, and the school is not yet rich enough to do so. He is allowed to attend all sorts of classes in the morning: at the age of fourteen he finds he prefers science to languages, and determines to become a doctor. At the same time he is admitted as a Grecian. He must still continue under the old system and work at science in the morning and receive his general education in the afternoon. It is obvious we can only teach him some of the things we teach to Auberon, so we choose for him the lightest and most amusing parts of general education, encourage him to read English and French, and to listen to music, of which he is very fond; and he accompanies us on those excursions into pure reason the nature of which we will hereafter explain; but we do not worry him with such difficult subjects as Latin and Greek. We hope he will be no worse a doctor and no less happy a man for having once taken interest in things quite outside his profession.

"Jack's parents are very poor indeed; as a matter of fact they are grocers in a small way, living at Kensal Rise. Yet Jack also is one of our most charming and intelligent boys. We have given him a scholarship at school, but we cannot, unfortunately, support him throughout life. We must assign him a profession, and we choose for him the profession of classical scholarship as being one of those in which a man may continue the pursuit of pure learning. He will obviously profit by the same Latin and Greek classes which Auberon and his fortunate companions attend in the mornings (these classes will be in the mornings, I say, for the sake of the many people like Arthur who are spending the morning in the professional work and have no time to spend on such a difficult subject as classical learning, but are ready to join their fellow Grecians in the afternoon). But Jack will not be with Auberon for more than the morning hour which he devotes to classics. Instead of sharing his lectures on European history and art, he will be working at the writing of Greek and Latin compositions and unravelling the mysteries of classical philology and grammar. We never let him cram for his scholarship, yet he obtains it, which is very surprising.

"Montague is like Auberon, the son of a rich nobleman, but he has inherited from his family an almost ineradicable stupidity. He brightens up a little, however, when we talk to him about railway engines and motor boats. We frankly tell the duke that we cannot give his son a good general education because he is incapable of profiting by it, but that we could turn him into a tolerable engineer. The angry peer takes his son away from us and sends him to Eton to learn the Latin genders after writing an indignant letter to the "Times" about our old English traditions and the value of gentlemen. Montague subsequently enters Parliament and becomes a prominent high churchman.

"Peter's father is a decayed tradesman; and as Peter is not a very brilliant boy, and never becomes a Grecian, all he can hope for, unless we help him, is to become a decayed tradesman in his turn. Peter, however, is quite good at mathematics and longs to be a surveyor. If we can, we help him to become one, on the understanding that he will repay us in future days when he is earning a good income. Though we have made no contract with him, contracts with minors being invalid, Peter has old-fashioned notions about what is honourable, and repays us as soon as he is able.

"Tom's father, never a rich man, dies, leaving nothing for Tom, who is a hopeless donkey. We do not cut Tom adrift, but procure for him a position on a ranch where his athletic prowess will stand him in good stead. Poor Tom!

"Having now suggested by these many examples more clearly, I think, than I could have done by pages of rules and explanations the sort of way in which various boys will be treated in our school, I will now pass on directly to explain that course of education which Auberon will follow, and which will occupy both his mornings and his afternoons as soon as he has (perhaps at the age of fifteen) passed the examination which admits him a Grecian.

"In doing so I shall refer from time to time to the beginnings of this education—to the sort of study which occupied Auberon's afternoons before he became a Grecian; but on the whole I think I may leave the details of his early education in the humanities to common sense.

"The first point I want to emphasize is that we intend to assign various importance to the various branches of knowledge, of which I hold some to be of far greater value than others.

"First and above all things our guardians must be philosophers. The world needs men who think clearly, who consider facts in their just proportion to the universe, who are not carried away by winds of doctrine, who can laugh the laugh of knowledge at epoch-making thoughts from Buda-Pesth or at scientific excursions into Christian apologetics.

"Yet I do not think it will be necessary to weary any boy who has not a special love of philosophy with the details of the history of thought, or of the hundred systems of a hundred philosophers. Certain books, indeed, he must peruse to sharpen his critical faculties. But instead of worrying him with the monads of Leibniz or with the premature and cryptic utterances of Thales and Heraclitus, instead of expecting him to grasp the curious theories of Avicenna, Hutchinson, and Hobbes, we will teach him Plato, Aristotle, Kant, and some modern philosophies, not that he may believe, but that he may ponder; and at evening in the shady garden overlooking the sea the Grecians will assemble round their Socrates for earnest discussion. This will be no neo-pagan revival, but a real continuation of the work attempted in the Academy of Athens. Moreover, we will permit all manner of men to come and talk to our boys, since thus only can we prepare them for a life in the course of which they will hear so many conflicting doctrines. Pragmatists shall address them with urgent persuasion on their lips; parsons shall work on their tender emotions and threaten them with the wrath of God; veiled mystics of the East shall expound the Sufic ecstasy or the Buddhist Nirvana, or exhibit the results of that antique process, salvation through starvation, to their shuddering gaze. Are not our pupils ΦΥΛΑΚΕΣ? Are they not Grecians? In the evening we will discuss quietly together the Pragmatist, the Parson, and the Hindu.

"But I am afraid a loud outcry will rise up against us from the virtuous of this world. 'What about their morals? You are sapping their morals, unholy corrupters of youth! You deserve the hemlock. Insist on a religion for them, insist at least on the Kantian categorical imperative, unless you desire your boys to re-enact the worst crimes of the house of Borgia.'

"But having a little moral shame ourselves we do not teach them creeds in which we do not believe in order to save ourselves trouble; and we refuse in our talks on philosophy to leave the categorical imperative uncriticized. We teach our boys to think about ethical problems, and a person not religiously inclined might even think it was more moral to think deeply about morality, and to take some trouble to form an individual code of ethics, than to take the whole matter on trust from parents or priests. And the result of our boldness will perhaps not be so very dreadful. Intelligent young men (as far as my university experience goes) are seldom bestial or outrageous in their desires, and, curious to relate, I have known hundreds of delightful people who have lived the most refined, elegant, and humane lives without the aid of religion or even of ethics.

"But the pure philosopher is not a sufficient ideal. We may find, we often do find, that such a man is wanting in several respects. In resolution, in power of command, in ability to deal with a crisis he may fail; but we must confess that no mental education can form these high qualities. For them we must look to a boy's natural endowments, and perhaps to the physical training he receives; and to test them we must consider his influence with others. But we may also find a pure philosopher very deficient in his appreciation of the joy of life: and education can do something for him here. For the joy of life is not to be understood by the reading of Norwegian drama, but is the heritage of those who have unlocked the secret door that leads into the garden of the senses.

"Hateful to me are those ignorant and thoughtless people who say that taste has no rules and that art cannot be taught: never did a more pernicious heresy flourish. It is quite true that we cannot inspire the blind with a passion for Rembrandt, or cause the mentally deranged to read Shakespeare with delight. But one can always take an intelligent boy (I speak from experience) and teach him first of all the history of art; and in the next place one can teach him to read, look, or listen with observation and intelligence. During this time, while he is acquiring what we may call artistic experience, he will have become vaguely appreciative. Now and only now is the time to instruct him in the principles of aesthetic law. For such law exists: it is not a mere matter of individual taste whether Velazquez be a better artist than Marcus Stone or not; or Milton greater than Keble or Vaughan. Velazquez *is* a better artist than Mr. Stone. The law is a complicated law, of course, but to consider its principles will be helpful; and it is refreshing for those who are bewildered by the disagreement of aesthetic experts to note that the greater knowledge those experts have, the more striking is their agreement in matters of appreciation.

"The three great arts I would place in this order of educational importance—literature, representation, music. I know there are some who consider music to be the purest and best of arts, because it requires for its comprehension no external intellectual effort, but makes a direct appeal to the emotions. The justice of this contention depends on our ideal of an art: that music has less *educational* importance than the two other sister arts becomes obvious if we admit the contention of those who make this lofty claim for music. For the understanding of a picture we require our previous observation of tangible objects, perhaps an appreciation of the value and expression of human emotions, certainly a subtle sympathy with a period of the world's art, life, and manners. But it is literature which appeals especially to educators as being always a criticism of life, however incomplete we may feel that definition to be: through reading literature we enhance our delight in life.

"We must therefore give our boys the most complete literary training possible, not often worrying them by examinations and commentaries, nor ever dreaming to make them acquainted with all the great books of the world before the age of twenty-one. Instead we shall permit them to read in a pleasant library, and give them advice or organize competitions in special subjects from time to time. I see no reason why Grecians or any other boys should ever be allowed to read perfectly worthless tales of adventure and magazine stuff, except to find therein examples of bad style and stupidity. This I suggest in no puritan spirit, with the idea that tales of pure delight or adventure are in themselves evil, but because England has produced Anthony Hope, Maurice Hewlett, Gilbert Chesterton among her minor writers of romance, not to mention those truly great narrators of splendid and exciting tales—Stevenson, Kipling, and Conrad. Of poetry also our boys must read the best. We will not give even our youngest boys inferior or so-called patriotic poetry to read, out of the false conception that such despicable stuff is specially suitable to a childish understanding. Yet though we will keep away from them the 'May Queen,' 'Casabianca,' and the 'Battle of the Baltic,' we will certainly enliven the interest of the young in verse by giving them to read such good stories as 'Sohrab and Rustum,' 'Enid and Geraint,' or the 'White Ship.' We shall teach them, moreover, that there are other beauties in poetry beyond metrical swing, and neither in reading English nor in reading classical verse shall boys, once the metre is mastered, ever be allowed to read to the obvious tramp of metre in a boarding-school sing-song style. It is so easy to make them read with more application of the refinements of poetic stress. Nor shall we fall into the opposite error and let them imagine, like our great actors, that blank verse should be read like prose. But they shall read with dignity, slowly, with realization of the beauty of each word, and of how in verse each word has its value, not only of sense, but of sound and association: they shall pause at the end of the lines and mark the metre subtly and not grossly: and all this may be taught to the wise.

"We will train our Grecian in the perception of different styles by giving them exercises to write in the varying styles of our English authors. We expect boys to write mock Cicero and Tacitus; why, in the name of common sense, can they not write mock Gibbon or Carlyle? Nor do I think for a minute that these exercises will hinder any from forming in later years an original style, but rather the reverse should happen, for boys so instructed will very clearly understand before they leave us that style is attained by scrupulous care and individuality of expression. In the same way we shall write English, not Greek or Latin, poetry, and, strange to say, we shall take these compositions more and not less seriously than the classical verse is taken now. We shall not give a prize once a year for some absurd heroics on a set theme, but we shall very diligently teach the art of verse, initiating our boys by setting them to write verse translations from poems in other tongues. Our criticism will be ruthless : we shall point out vulgarity of idea, insufficiency of thought, staleness of metaphor, harshness of sound. We shall not necessarily produce great poets by this training, but we shall certainly produce young men who love poetry and (what is rarer still) who understand it. The artist may have an incomplete understanding of poetry ; but only the artist can have a complete understanding of it.

"It is here that we must consider which dead or

living tongues our guardians must know, for we shall consider at present the learning of a language merely as a means of reading a new literature. Latin and Greek are inevitable, both from the intrinsic merit of their literature and from the force of the historical tradition which Edwinson once so fluently pointed out. But our teaching of these languages will be revolutionary except in the case of those boys who are taking them as part of their technical training in order to win university scholarships. There will be no writing, and certainly (if Dr. Rouse will forgive us) no speaking, of Latin and Greek. We shall let such portions of the grammar as are not very important (genders and the parts of Latin verbs) be rather learnt in the course of reading than laboriously committed to memory. We shall read very quickly in class, and confine ourselves to works which are either good in themselves, historically interesting, or influential on subsequent thought. We shall divert the young with Homer, easiest of great poets, with Lucian's ' Vera Historia,' with a few legends of old Rome from Livy, and with fairy tales from Apuleius. We will not weary even Grecians with Thucydides when he talks about dreary expeditions into Ætolia; but all Grecians shall read the fate of the Sicilian expedition, and learn by heart the speech of Pericles. Into Demosthenes we will only dip ; of Sophocles and Euripides we will select the finest plays and read them, as well as the Æschylean trilogy, more than once. Herodotus we shall read through lightly, as is fitting, and we shall take parts in the plays of Aristophanes in merry congress; of Plato we shall never weary, for he is good for the soul. Nor shall we presume to forget Theocritus and the lyric fragments, or those unfading roses of the Anthology which tell how roses fade. And only for the very young shall we Bowdlerize anything, since we are dealing, not with urchins, but with the select and chosen few.

"In Latin we will trouble no reasonable soul with Plautus and Terence, or with more of Cicero than is needed to grasp the excellent style of that second-rate intellect. Of Ovid, too, who is only interesting when immoral, we shall read, for the style's sake, some of the duller portions. To the claims of those deathless school-books, the Æneid of Virgil, the Odes of Horace, and the Satires of Juvenal, we shall submit, for their fame is deserved; Lucretius and Catullus are too obvious to mention; Tibullus is a sleepy fellow; and from Propertius we select. Tacitus tells us much history and is pleasant to read, nor are the letters of Pliny the Younger disagreeable; but Caesar I would abandon to the historical specialist, and Livy I would read in haste. Of Apuleius only one book is essentially disagreeable; the rest is charming, and too long neglected.

"Now the total bulk of all that I have commended as readable in these two languages is not very large, and could easily be stowed away into some twenty well-printed volumes. As soon as the preliminaries are mastered we shall read through the classics for three hours a week for three years. No boy except the specialist shall begin Latin or Greek till he is fifteen years old; this will ensure, I think, that he does not waste about five years in learning grammar, but attacking a not very difficult subject at a riper age, will master it within a quarter of the time it would have taken him had he, after the usual school fashion, begun Latin at the age of nine and Greek at the age of eleven. He should therefore be ready at the age of sixteen for our three years' classical course, and though we shall not spend anything like as much time over the classics as do other schools which are still hampered by the Renaissance and scholastic traditions, and by external examinations, I believe our boys will love the classics more and obtain a fuller understanding of the classical spirit than those to whom Latin and Greek are a ceaseless drudgery and evil. I believe they will learn, no less than others have learnt, from these time-honoured studies, that calm and even fervour of mind, that sane and serene love of beautiful things, that freedom from religious bigotry and extravagance which marks the writings of the Greeks, and that seriousness, decorum, and strength, that sense of arrangement and justice which marks the writings and still more the history of the Romans.

"We have now to consider in how many modern European tongues we are going to give universal instruction, not forgetting that our Grecians are going to have so much time to themselves, so many hours when they are simply to go into the library and read, that it will be easy for us to encourage and help any boy of linguistic ability who, discontented with what

we can teach him, desires to enrich his knowledge of
those languages he learns in school, or to attempt
some rarer and more exciting tongue—Spanish
Swedish, Russian, or even Persian, fired perhaps by
the eloquence of some literary specialist, whom we
have invited to lecture at the school, and his trans-
lated extracts. But I may surprise some if I say at
the outset, that I cannot consider that there is any
but the slightest educational value in the actual ac-
quisition of a modern language, in learning to speak
it, read it, or write it, apart from the serious study of
the literature, history, and traditions of a foreign
people. Any German clerk, as Hofman remarked
when he so briefly dismissed those who suggested
that a good modern language education was a fine
practical thing, any cosmopolitan or Swiss innkeeper,
any half-breed dragoman can gabble six or seven
tongues, and sometimes gabble them correctly; and
the dreariest lady student from Russia can speak
beautiful French and passable German, and yet not
have in her head a single Russian, not to speak of a
German or French, idea.

"Nevertheless, very fine is the spirit of the true
linguist, which I admit to be a very different thing
from the mere spirit of literary curiosity which desires
to learn just enough of a language to read some
favourite or famous author in the original. The true
linguist revels in fantastic grammars where the verbs
open out in the middle to make themselves passive
or negative, and numerals agree with singular mascu-
line nouns in the genitive feminine plural. He delights

in learning and in reproducing curious scripts whose mysterious systems of dots, segmented circles, or paint-brush strokes have charmed his eye. He revels in making obscure noises foreign to the English ear, and in planning out euphonic changes and philological laws. If we have a boy filled with this spirit among our Grecians we shall be delighted, we shall provide him with all manner of grammars and dictionaries, and persuade his parents to send him abroad for the summer holidays to perfect himself.

"But we shall not have the time nor the inclination to devote such special attention to the three languages, French, German, and Italian, which we hope to teach regularly to all our Grecians. We shall learn to translate from these languages, and to pronounce them fairly correctly when we read them aloud. To attain this pronunciation we shall most certainly not employ the ridiculously complicated script of the International Phonetic Association, realizing as we do that the only European language for the learning of which the employment of a phonetic script is necessary is English: French, German, and Italian, at all events, are pronounced almost entirely as they are written. What is the use, sense, or wisdom of having a sign like a broken hoop ᴐ to represent the final *o* of Italian, and therefore forcing the miserable boys to learn two methods of writing every time they learn a language, when it is so extremely easy to tell him that the final Italian *o* is often sounded like the English *o* in not? The refinements of pronunciation can be learnt at any time by any one who has a good ear, and who already knows the language pretty well, by a few months' stay in a foreign country; and a boy can go abroad, after all, at any period of his life. I admit that to attain this final perfection a knowledge of phonetic laws and the use of plaster casts of throats and larynxes may be recommended, but these devices are indescribably pernicious when employed in the instruction of beginners. They are the conceited invention of modern science, which, in its desire that we should scorn useless knowledge and become practical, would have us spend six years in acquiring a fine French accent in England, without leaving us time to read a word of Molière. In the early stages of instruction in French I admit that the use of such an entirely rational and immediately comprehended script as that invented for the Faculté of Grenoble may be attended with profit, constructed as it is for the French language alone instead of being a complicated scientific universal affair which one can fit on to Czech and Turkish. This script from Grenoble clearly shows how words should be run together in reading French sentences, and how the accent and pause must come after groups of words pronounced without a break; yet it can be learnt in ten minutes. Next I admit that the teacher must be a master of French sound: I do not think it, however, at all advisable that he should be a Frenchman, although we may at all times call in a native to read to us or talk with us. An Englishman who with toil has acquired a fine French accent, knows the difficulties with which the English boy has to contend so much better; he only will understand English as well as French phonetics; he will be able to explain that o and e are diphthongs in English without getting into a towering rage at the stupidity and perverseness of the English boy, and if he is wise he will appeal to the boys to remember how a Frenchman talks English— an obvious way of getting boys to be interested in the pronunciation of French, yet which seems never to have occurred to any teachers.

" We shall hardly attempt to teach boys to talk or write these languages, unless they are especially interested in so doing; and if they are, we shall only teach them to talk and write French. This may displease some, but there are obvious reasons for our decision. Firstly, to learn a language so as to be able to go abroad and ask for a ticket at the station and a drink at the café is obviously part of technical training, and not worthy the attention of serious educationalists. Secondly, an intelligent boy, if he wants to talk, must go to France, where in a family he will learn more in a week than we could teach him in a year. The true educational value of talking a language consists in getting the ear attuned to subtle, new, and delicate sounds, and this we preserve by emphasizing the necessity of reading it aloud.

" We shall perhaps then spend a little time in French conversation, viewing it not as an end, but as a means towards eradicating that awkward shyness, which some of the most pleasant and intelligent young Englishmen feel at opening their mouths before foreigners. But how much better it would be if we could send them abroad for a month a year to talk with French, German, and Italian boys, to view the beauties and delights of foreign towns, foreign institutions, and foreign manners, if we could arrange for them to have some one better than the usual dreary *pasteur* or *pfarrer* to talk with, and to hear lectures by the most famous foreign teachers. If we were rich enough or powerful enough to institute this *wanderjahr* system for our boys, our training in modern languages would then become one of the most important and fascinating parts of their education.

"But if we cannot do this, we can initiate them into these three great literatures, and we can teach them to read foreign books, not at the rate of a page an hour, but swiftly and with pleasure. You may perhaps be a little surprised if I tell you on what part of French literature we shall lay greatest stress. For we shall not read very much French lyric poetry: admirable as it is, its educational value is not very large to those who have read classical and English lyric verse. We shall follow consistently our plan of giving boys a pleasant introduction to subjects in which they may specialize afterwards if they will, and we will make no attempt to get them to read through all that is important in French lyrical verse, or, indeed, in any other branch of literature. Perhaps we shall do well if we confine ourselves to the 'Oxford Book of French Verse': it is a tolerable anthology, not much superior in anything but length to that admirable sixpenny 'Cent Meilleurs Poèmes,' and woefully inferior to that splendid collection, the

'Oxford Book of English Verse.' If we consider
further what French lyric author a boy would do well
to read through, I can think of none better than
Leconte de Lisle: there is no more suitable book for
boys in French than his clear and powerful ' Poèmes
Barbares.'

"We shall omit Erckmann-Chatrian's ' Waterloo '
and the good but second-rate ' Colomba ' from our
course, and no more dream of giving young boys
Corneille and Racine than we would dream of
trying to interest a Frenchman in English by pre-
senting him with ' Paradise Lost.' At first we shall
read such diverting and interesting books as ' Le
Bourgeois Gentilhomme,' ' Les Trois Mousquetaires,'
' Le Crime de Silvestre Bonnard,' and certain selected
short stories. But it is the great French novelists who
should be most esteemed by those who are training
boys over seventeen years of age to face a world far
less pleasant than our school. Only Hardy and
Meredith among our so delightful English writers can
ever impress the awakening mind so deeply with the
tragic realities and possibilities of existence as do
' Père Goriot,' ' Madame Bovary,' ' Une Vie,' and
' Pierre et Jean,' books in which the ugliness of life is
faced and the psychology of passion analysed, yet
written at the inspiration of an ideal which is the
more impressive because it is unconscious and full of
the sense that a good deal is worth doing for its own
sake, even if it be unromantic and unknown. To be
recommended, too, are the quiet, humorous, thoughtful
books of Anatole France, that gentleman Socialist,

whose graceful and bitter laughter reviles a world
gone mad, a world which it is our fond dream to
better by producing some half dozen young men a
year who are fit to face it.

"We shall not need so much German as French,
for the language is far harder, and the literature, the
importance of which is only a hundred years old, far
less important. I shall be contented if we read in
school the first part of 'Faust,' the songs of Heine,
part of Benzmann's 'Collection of Modern German
Lyrics.' In reading German, Jean Paul, Sudermann,
and Nietzsche should not be neglected, for Nietzsche
has an influence which all thoughtful men should
understand, however much they may hate him, and a
style second to none in German. Freytag and
Grillparzer and other pompous triflers we shall
neglect; but we shall remember that Heine wrote
prose hardly inferior to his verse. We must attach,
however, far more importance to the language of the
Germans than their purely literary achievements
could warrant. All boys who are interested in science,
art, or archaeology will soon find out that they must
be able to read the barbarous prose of this most
educated and learned people, since in every branch of
pure learning the Germans have produced some
master work, some 'epoch-making' treatise.

"Italian we shall reinvest with the honour and importance which it has so unjustly lost since the first
half of the nineteenth century. In the days of Peacock
no gentleman with any pretension of culture could
afford to dispense with a smattering of this delightful

tongue, whose literature we now imagine to be represented by Dante, Petrarch, and the ' Promessi Sposi '
of Manzoni. It is sad to think that there are now not
a hundred living Englishmen who know and enjoy
the calm and classic humour of Ariosto, or who care
anything for the countless masters of early Italian
lyrical verse, which Eugenia Levi has collected in
her two fascinating volumes. Yet no classical scholar
can be excused for not taking the trouble to learn to
read this easiest of languages, when a fortnight's work
will enable him to read any average Italian prose with
fluency and enjoyment.

"Our boys shall know a great deal of Dante, a
little of Petrarch, the two great collections of Italian
verse to which we have referred, besides a little
anthology by Carducci, which extends to the nineteenth century; nor shall they neglect to read the
splendid 'Barbarous Odes' of Carducci himself, which,
based on the Horatian metres, form so brave a protest
against the natural deficiency of a tongue wherein
rhymes are too easy and compression too hard.
Several of the tales of Boccaccio, even some of Bandello
and Masuccio claim consideration, for they do not
all consist, as some imagine, of indecent ribaldry, but
are full of pathos, humour, and most cunning psycho-
logical observation; and why neglect the ' Cortigiano'?
Our playwrights shall be Goldoni and D'Annunzio:
perhaps not the D'Annunzio of the terrible 'Città
Morta,' but certainly the D'Annunzio of ' Francesca
da Rimini.' For are we not the heirs of the Italian
Renaissance, and shall we continue to neglect a

literature not inferior to the French and far greater than the German, a literature which in the present age has produced at least two immortal names? Least of all can we dream of so doing after gazing at the masterpieces of Italian painting. Would it not be well to know what these great men read, thought, and wrote? Have we forgotten that Italy is also the first, and will perhaps be the last, home of the purest and most noble music? To understand the spirit of the greatest artistic country the world has ever known, greater in my opinion than Greece herself by virtue of Leonardo and Michelangelo, not to mention Scarlatti and Pergolese, is surely the direct duty of any one who desires to enjoy all that life can offer, and to assist others to share his delight.

"We must now consider the arts of representation, instruction in which will be such a peculiar and delightful feature of our school. We must adopt in teaching this subject methods similar to those we adopted for teaching poetry. I mean that we must not begin by laying down aesthetic laws, but by considering art historically. Numerous photographs, reproductions and casts must adorn our buildings or fill our portfolios. We must show magic-lantern slides, and we must take our boys to visit the great galleries at London and Hampton Court; and in this way we must form, as far as residents in England can do so, the basis of artistic experience. We shall have three direct ways of training our boys; they must notice things in pictures, they must regard nature from an artistic point of view, and they must attempt to represent things for themselves. However clumsy their efforts be, every boy must draw and paint for at least three hours a week, not copying absurd patterns, but inventing for himself or imitating nature. Our object in this our practice of art, as in practice of poetry, will not be to train up artists—though who knows whether some young Velazquez will not suddenly discover his powers in this way?—but to enable boys to appreciate art, technically and soundly. Those who would be artists or architects must have special morning training for their professions. At all events we will have no sonneteering about art in the windbag style of John Addington Symonds, no vain talk of the grandeur, sweet loveliness, invincible truth, and tragic terror of pictures. We shall study rather to ensure a minute trained observation into shades of style and variations of detail ; for only in this way can we teach boys not naturally artists to perceive every portion of a picture and not its subject alone. We shall also—and this will be a most important part of our pictorial education—take bad and popular modern works—Luke Fildes' ' Doctor,' or Dicksee's picture of the knight impressed by the crucifix—as examples of inferior art, and point out in these either the defects of drawing and colour or the complete inanity and vulgarity of idea.

" The introduction of this artistic education I consider the most revolutionary, the most important, of new proposals. It may interest you to know that I was for some time both at Oxford and Cambridge. I must have known some three hundred undergraduates, most of whom were considered or considered themselves to be the most intelligent young Englishmen of the day. Yet I do not remember more than four or five of them who could have told a Signorelli from a Titian, or who have ever heard the name of Pisanello. To possess any knowledge of art was considered by my otherwise intelligent friends to be something rather extraordinary and priggish. Perhaps, indeed, the character of an undergraduate art-lover would be bound to suffer in so philistine an atmosphere. Yet there is no happier man than he who loves painted things, for the whole realm of nature becomes exalted in his eyes: he looks at the world, and imagines great pictures in his soul, he looks at great pictures and begins to realize the unspeakable beauty of the world. And what is Greece to those who do not love the sweet spring of her vases and the immortal strength of her statuary? How can men appreciate the great life of the modern world without knowing something of Manet, Pisarro, Whistler, and all those once obscure heroes who, despite penury and starvation, imprisoned the wonders of bright light on painted canvas? A few Japanese prints, or Persian miniatures, or Indian bronzes—are these not the only things that can suggest to us, who cannot read those literatures or voyage to those lands, the marvels of each racial individuality? Yet in our public schools, where still so much of the true humane education lingers, the artistic life is entrusted to some ill-paid pedagogue who has drawn a little at the Slade School, and is usually considered to be rather inferior in intellectual ability and social standing to the other members of the staff. It is, perhaps, the worst mistake in English public-school life, for even those boys who learn drawing and excel in it will never get any real encouragement or help.

" I confess that my enthusiasm for music is not so great as my enthusiasm for the arts of representation. I have known only too many good musicians, especially those who were simply good performers, who outside this one specialized atmosphere were not only stupid, but exhibited the most appalling mental vulgarity. I do not view with favour perpetual toil on iron-frame pianos ; I should like to leave the performance of instrumental music solely to those who show their love and capability—and musical genius is always revealed early in life. But every boy as soon as his voice is set, or before it breaks, might learn to read music and to sing in part ; and one could have, at least once a fortnight, a concert for the hearing of which some boys would have been prepared by giving them the scores to read and explaining the modulations and subtleties of the tune. This is never done : the consequence is, intelligent boys who have not exceptional gifts, usually prefer the vilest musical comedy to Mozart. It is not they are deaf to sounds as a rule, but simply that they have no conception of the aim and structure of classical music.

" We have considered the education we intend to give in philology and fine arts. We must still examine whether we are to teach history, mathematics, and science.

" We shall have little difficulty in settling the place

of history in our routine. No study seems more specious as a substitute for liberal education in the arts; yet it is dangerous to view it too seriously or give it too much importance. History is a fascinating tale which should be read only in the works of a great prose writer who is capable of doing it justice; but it is a story with so little of moral or of meaning, a story which may well make us discontented sceptics, and cause us to despair of the progress of mankind. For philosophies of history have not succeeded: not even Hegel could thread together the promiscuous events of the world's life into a connected whole.

"We say this, however, only as a warning to those who are too enthusiastic, or who imagine that the study of the historical method has a supreme value in education. It is obvious that our Grecians must have such acquaintance with history, and especially with modern history, as will enable them to understand the political life of the present and the artistic life of the past. It is obvious that it will be good for them to read, not in class perhaps, but to themselves, such noble books as Gibbon, Mommsen, 'Italy and her Invaders,' or Fyffe's 'History of Modern Europe'; obvious that since they have to read Herodotus, Thucydides, and Tacitus, we shall teach them in reference to these authors some of the latest results of historical research. Yet we need seldom insist on their learning dates and sketching out the plans of battles, nor shall we fatigue them with the history of the dull periods of the world. But in their last year at school those young men of twenty who are likely to be directly interested in the government of our country must specialize in modern history, in state theory, and in the science of economics.

"But we shall find history most useful as a pleasant and instructive afternoon diversion for those not very intelligent boys who are working to enter a trade or profession; it is perhaps the simplest and most obvious method of inducing an ordinary mind to be interested in an extraneous world, for the very reason that it is too shallow a subject to have a prime importance in the higher education.

"I would suggest that our Grecians be compelled to learn sufficient mathematics to prevent their being put to shame in the affairs of life, and no more, unless they specially desire it. That a training in pure mathematics has an educational value I readily admit: it is beneficial if a boy be clever enough to apply mathematical principles to argument and discussion. But neither is it necessary to become an abstruse or advanced mathematician in order to be able to apply the elementary mathematical law, nor do boys who are trained in philosophical thought need to acquire the principles of logic by such circuitous means.

"Of the teaching of elementary arithmetic and geometry to the ordinary or young boy, we have already dealt with Hofman's aid; and I am thankful to say that there are distinct signs that our educationalists are weary of stocks, discount, and wall-papering. We have suggested that the younger boys will delight in working out the problems of simple geometry for themselves when they measure, buy, and design their wood constructions in the workshop. We hope that our Grecians will perpetuate a love for manual craft of this kind: that they will long to construct ambitious models, to design furniture worthy of their artistic training, to paper their own rooms, and bind their own books. For not even the physical exercise which compels them to measure themselves in that athletic prowess for which a boy always has been and always will be most admired by his fellows will have a more salutary effect than the patient toil of saw and plane in keeping them from priggishness and from any form of dreamy, intellectual superiority. Shall we let those whom we are training to be rulers be so stupid or haughty that they will have to sit still in cushioned seats, while a hired mechanic repairs the incorrigible car?

"These remarks refer to applied science as much as to applied mathematics. But we must return a moment to the study of pure mathematical theory. We must hope to find a wonderful teacher who will suggest the mystery and charm of numbers to his pupils without, perhaps, directly saying a word about that mystery and charm; who will recognize that even among Grecians not one boy in a hundred is likely to become a great mathematician, and will therefore make no attempt to weary his class by forcing them to work out innumerable examples, but rather hope to interest them in the delight he himself takes in mathematical problems, by selecting the most fascinating and important examples of mathematical method.

"Natural science must now be our most difficult consideration. Science is an exacting mistress, and if I decide that we shall not insist on our Grecians penetrating its glorious secrets, let no one think that I say this in a spirit of hostility or contempt, least of all while I sit here in view of Florence and remember that her triumphs of art are triumphs not of a mere vague aesthetic delight, but of inquisitive, patient, universal research into the nature of things and into the hidden laws of the world. By scientific study, Uccello learnt the joys of perspective, Signorelli some—alas, not all!—of the secrets of anatomy, Brunelleschi the architectural principle which enabled him to construct that huge and splendid dome that stands so quiet and impressive in the last hours of this far-shadowing afternoon.

"Yet science brooks no rival in her house; he who would follow her must abandon other joys and spend long hours with her alone. To suggest to our Grecians the charms and delights of science will be our duty, but those who would set about to perfect themselves therein must do so in after years. But I will, at all events, give no countenance to the foolish and vulgar hostility with which so-called classical men too often treat science and her followers, though one can easily explain to them their foolish error. They see that the youth of England, with its puritan hatred of the useless and beautiful, strong in its all-pervading and plebeian common sense, has devoted itself to natural science with barbaric vigour. Also they have observed with disgust that even the oldest and firmest established homes of classical learning cannot entirely resist the clamour for a more profitable and vital course of instruction, that many of their pupils have abandoned the dissection of Latin periods for the dissection of flowers and corpses. Therefore it is that so many second-rate and a few first-rate, but narrow classical scholars, have raised this most vulgar outcry against the vulgarity of science, not perceiving that they are confusing science with a section of her followers. Was Leonardo vulgar?

"Natural science, unaccompanied by other studies, is a poor training for the mind, though I can conceive it to be a far better one than these arid pedants could possibly give with their syntax and paradigms. Scientific men are so often headstrong in their own conceit: they are fond of laying down the law on subjects they have not attempted to master; and some of them, like Nordau, have the impertinence to pose as authorities on morality, aesthetics, and religion. The opinions and arguments of scientific men seldom rise above the level of a childish materialism which any serious philosopher could disprove in two minutes: they are utterly incapable of clear thought, yet imagine that philosophers must be muddle-headed because they are not persuaded by their 'common-sense' arguments. Furthermore, they are either neglectful or contemptuous of most artistic life, though they are often fine musicians. A refined man, I admit, will never become vulgarized by science, but it seems very clear that science can never refine the vulgar.

"I do not think, then, that my Grecians will be

expected to do more than attend two weekly lectures delivered in non-technical language on scientific laws. The enthusiasts may work as much as they want: we shall provide laboratories, and specially encourage, perhaps, some of the less difficult branches of scientific study. I do not think, moreover, that our school museum will contain such a collection of riff-raff as may usually be found in those primitive establishments—bowls from Palestine, a pipe from Russia, specimens of Swiss pottery and Indian shells, a cork model of the Coliseum, twenty ill-stuffed birds under glass, and a photograph of the moon. We will attempt rather to give our museum a real and systematic interest, not crowding it with ethnological specimens unless we can afford a magnificent number, but rather priding ourselves on our neat and systematic collection of local flora and fauna.

"We have now considered the higher education. A word remains to be said on some few miscellaneous points.

"We have not mentioned the education of women. I do not think either the advantages or the dangers of co-educational schools are very great. The presence of girls certainly tends to prevent a boy from inclining to certain perversions, but it cannot be doubted that there is a grandeur and beauty about our monastic schools which the presence of women would destroy; and if one observes those who have been brought up in co-educational schools one is very apt to find them over-sentimental or otherwise eccentric. I think the girls reap practically all the benefit.

"I would rather women were educated by themselves, but I fear the inferiority of the female schoolmistress, and, indeed, of the female mind, is so great that they will never be educated as our Grecians are. For the ideal education for a woman would be exactly the education we give our Grecians—with a most special and most severe stress laid on philosophy and on free thought, in order to eradicate the sentimental viciousness of the sex; and women must learn, above all, to read their books unexpurgated without losing the modesty of youth—yet this, it seems, a boy can do often, and a woman never. Have we not seen that greatest of girls' schools in the west of England? Have we not remarked its sumptuous buildings, pseudo-antique, asymmetrical, gaudily tricked out in the most execrable taste? Have we not seen girls who have never heard of Augustus or Velazquez, and could not see through a leading article, plodding through Beowulf, learning by heart their German grammar, acting before admiring friends such masterpieces of English literature as Charles Kingsley's 'Saint's Tragedy,' and amusing themselves with chip carving? Did not that truly great woman who achieved so much in the emancipation of her sex from a tradition which permitted them to study little but singing and deportment, write down that Latin was dangerous for girls to read, and commend the bracing effect of Hebrew and German poetry (Schiller's 'Glocke,' forsooth, or the 'Faust' seduction scene, I wonder)? It is a pity, for where will our Grecians find women fit to be their life companions and friends?

" I might in this place make a brief observation with regard to day schools. There is only one argument that can be adduced in favour of day schools. They do not tend, like our great public schools, to create a monotonous type. Such an education as we should give would destroy the argument. To my mind the great curse of day schools is that boys should live perpetually with their parents. Only one parent in a thousand is fit to manage an intelligent boy. A boy may be bullied in school; it will be nothing to the way in which he will be bullied at home if he is ever so little exceptional, ever so little inclined to disagree with the parental outlook. Then, again, if he is punished at a day school it is immediately known at home; every little punishment is a punishment twice over. It is a horrible system, this ceaseless double supervision.

" I speak thus strongly not because I wish to break down family ties, but because I earnestly wish to preserve them. The boy who loves his parents rightly will be sad to leave them, rejoiced to find them again after many days. Their influence is deeper, finer, more pathetic when transmitted through loving letters and accepted in loving replies. The individual parent who, being human, must have foibles, is sunk in the ideal parent, the loving watcher over the destiny of his far-off child. Every honest man, recalling his own school days, will agree with me in this.

" Another point. If you think, as perhaps you do, that our education attempts too much, remember what we have cancelled from the ordinary sixth-form routine. Nearly all the preparation which occupies two hours every night is gone. All translation can be done very well unseen. Three hours a week for classics, three for drawing, an evening a week each for a philosophical discussion, a lecture in literature, a lecture in science or mathematics. Three hours each for reading the four great modern literatures; and three for the practice of English prose and verse. An hour for history, an hour a day in the library. Twenty-eight hours a week, excluding evenings. There is room to fill up what I have forgotten!

"We should next briefly consider the position our Grecians will occupy in school affairs. They will all be monitors, and no other boys, however successful athletically, however superior in character, will be given the honour. It is the tribute we shall pay in our school to intellectual pre-eminence, and only those who have been to a school which was ruled by the heroes of its Rugby football team can realize how admirable was the system which Arnold suggested. They will have the power of punishing other boys by giving them detention; the actual punishment will be inflicted in this way under the supervision of the masters: there will be no physical appeal against their authority. In a school of about five hundred boys we may hope for thirty Grecians. They will have a common room, will alone have private studies, will be allowed when they are over seventeen to smoke and drink wine in moderation, for it will be our policy to encourage them in self-restraint, not to put temptation out of the way. The rest of the school will not be divided into houses.

That is a pernicious system by which a boy only sees
some thirty of his fellows, and cannot get away from
the aggressiveness of those schoolfellows whom he
dislikes. We shall send our Grecians to keep order
throughout the school and in the dormitories (which
are to be open and not partitioned), and we hope in
this way to test and prove their powers of government.
Few realize or remember that it is much harder for
the unpopular boy to manage his fellows than for an
unpopular ministry to manage the State: no one is
more relentless, ingenious, persistent in hatred, than
the schoolboy who dislikes and despises those who
are set over him. Our Grecians will be allowed to
play games or not as they please, but we must insist
that the captain of games in the school be a Grecian
himself.

" I discussed with some impatience, if you remember,
those who desired us to give instruction in morals.
But that was not because we do not care about the
morals of our Grecians, but because my imaginary
objectors desired me to be immoral enough to tell them
lies. But not even a ΓΕΝΝΑΙΟΝ ΨΕΥΔΟΣ will be
admitted to defile the education of our Grecians, though
I am afraid we may have to talk dogmatically to the
rest of the school. The greatest moral influence that
the Grecians can possibly receive must be their own
tradition and public feeling, and the example of great
books and the deep friendship and respect they feel
for those high-principled men whom we hope to find
to teach them. We will not say to boys who are
reading Plato, 'God wrote down in a book that you

must not lie, therefore you will go to hell if you do so.' We will not say to them that happiness in this earth belongs to the moral. But we will say to them, 'The school, your kind mother and gentle guardian, hates the vulgar and sensual life, and detests that which is mean and false: hoc disce aut discede.' And though we will not be as ruthless as some are to the natural faults of the headstrong, generous, and warm-blooded youth, yet if we consider a Grecian, however intelligent, to be ineradicably coarse, dishonest, or mean, he shall not remain in our society.

" And the last and most important of our considerations is the schoolmaster. Yet, strange as it may seem at first, I do not despair of finding ardent, learned, and admirable young men at our universities who would far rather teach than become dons or Indian magistrates if we gave them a salary worth the name, assured them a pension, and treated them with honour. Too often the modern schoolmaster has to take up his profession because there is nothing better for him to do; he is consequently, and with some justice, supposed to be a man not clever enough to obtain a fellowship or not energetic enough to enter the State service; he is a social outcast or a social failure; he ranks with the curate: he is an ill-dressed, ill-shaved nonentity. Our masters will be at first men carefully chosen for their charm and intelligence, and not merely according to the results of their university work; later, the best of our old boys will rejoice to return to us and help us. Masters in La Giocosa are not treated as subordinates, but as honourable friends of the head master. They live with him, dine with him nightly, and fare with the best. They are men who do not imagine their education is complete; they are a band of older Grecians. They need not be mewed up within school walls for three-quarters of the year, but must have all the society they can find, every chance of visiting London, every opportunity of conversing with specialists who come to lecture, and the wise men and travellers who come to visit.

"I think, strange to say, we shall find it easy to find those who will adequately teach our earnest and gentle-mannered Grecians. Shall we give less honour to those who do the ceaseless drudgery and rough work of the school, who help the infants to write, and read, and add, or try to drive the foolish through accidence and syntax? Shall we not rather let our chief masters do this difficult, elementary, noble work in turn, and not attempt to maintain a staff of less clever, less refined and serious men for this the hardest portion of the school work?

"And the choice of masters and the success of the whole school must depend on one man, the grave and learned senior who is to be our head. Alas, that we cannot recall Vittorino from his grave! Yet if we could, what princes would send their sons to La Giocosa in these iron days? Who appreciates the humanities now apart from the picturesque dignity that hangs about them still? Who cares for any real thought about education? Who dares to make an ideal? Some listen to the conceited, lying scientist who writes pedantic treatises on habit, brain-formation, and memory, and veils his tired platitudes in the ugliest of technical terms—and here they fondly imagine lies the secret of success. Some are willing to let our old beautiful schools rot away till they become hotels where the newly-rich may consort with the mattoid nobleman; in foolish calm they await the time when a relentlessly progressive age will hurl them aside in disgust. Never do they attempt a reform which is to make them liker their true selves; but they cringe to public examinations and public feeling, and make each unworthy concession either with ill-grace or a puerile flourish of trumpets.

"But we will re-found La Giocosa, and build it anew in England beside the sea that typifies our race. And if I have made no single direct reference to patriotism, let me say this now. Patriotism is not taught by bad poetry and bad literature, by rifle clubs, or Union Jacks, or essays on Tariff Reform. La Giocosa will give England men of intelligence, fit to govern her, and not private soldiers fit to be shot down for her in some financial war. And in training Grecians La Giocosa has fulfilled her duty to England. Ours shall be no ideal school for the ideal youth, but a place where hard work is done, and where boys are toilfully prepared for the difficulties of a modern world; yet where, too, we shall train many to understand and love the sweet pleasures of the senses. We even hope that a few of our scholars will be among the great. Now, my friends, our long and toilsome journey is over: and it is evening."

Evening, indeed, had come and the cool hours of the day, but those two who listened to the unadorned words of this strange youth heard and understood the earnestness in his voice; and as they gazed at him while he lay there on the grass refolding his sheaf of papers, they thought of his gentle voice and eager words, and he seemed to them to be none other than one of his own Grecians, strayed from some Elysian school where Socrates and Vittorino teach and all the young lords of that shadow-world listen and admire. And whether their journey with him was ended, whether they would return to England to the old and weary toil strengthened by this secret and beautiful ideal, or whether they would not rather join him and rebuild La Giocosa to the sound of music in an Atlantean isle, in that swift minute of wonder they could hardly tell.

III

CRITICAL STUDIES

JOHN DAVIDSON: REALIST

A POINT OF VIEW

THREE moderns, Ibsen, Nietzsche, and John Davidson, all cry with one voice that as an antidote to our quiet, self-satisfied, ill-founded idealism, we require the great virtues of strength and self-realization. Indeed, they often forget that any other virtues have existence. Thus, Ibsen has portrayed Peer Gynt with an onion in his hand, peeling off husk after husk as he attempts by analogy to find his true self. Also he has told the tale of Brand, terrible idealist, destroying all that love him by his self-denying devotion to duty. Again, "Whoso loveth his God chastiseth him," this is the sneer of Nietzsche, who evolves the "Overman," whose strength justifies his power. And John Davidson, in a passage which may be considered the crude germ of everything he has done in Ballads, Eclogues, Songs, Plays, Testaments, makes Smith say to the woman he loves:

> Think my thought, be impatient as I am,
> Obey your Nature, not Authority;

and describes

> The hydra-headed creeds, the Sciences
> That deem the thing is known when it is named;

And Literature, Thought's palace-prison fair;
Philosophy, the grand inquisitor
That racks ideas and is fooled with lies;
Society, the mud wherein we stand. . . .

Of such extreme importance, then, is Mr. Davidson's outlook, and his criticism of life, that we shall best do him justice if we somewhat neglect the technical merits of his poetry, glancing at them rapidly, and passing on to his matter as soon as possible.

As a beautiful prelude I quote a lyric from "Scaramouch in Naxos":

The boat is chafing at our long delay,
    And we must leave too soon
The spicy sea-pinks and the inborne spray,
    The tawny sands, the moon.

Keep us, O Thetis, on our Western flight,
    Watch from thy pearly throne
Our vessel, plunging deeper into night
    To reach a land unknown.

Even the bare recital of these faultless lines, not to mention those already quoted from "Smith," are enough to show that, from the first, Mr. John Davidson was no minor poet.

The questions a critic must answer, if he would attempt to estimate his Author's rank, are—How lofty is his ambition? and, next, How far does he realize it? It seems to me that Mr. Davidson's ambition rivals that of any Author who ever took up pen to write. In fact, one sometimes has an uncomfortable feeling that he is not great enough to carry out his aims. But he so far succeeds that his imperfections surpass the perfections of other men. So we must deal with him as we would deal, say, with Keats, Shelley, or Tennyson.

First of all, then, we will acknowledge Mr. Davidson's faults. They are quite obvious, being chiefly due to a strained desire for simplicity, and to perpetual over-emphasis of his point. Sometimes he will spoil a ballad with lines too colloquial for the hurrying metre; sometimes he will just mar a fine speech in blank verse by getting it involved, and hard to follow, or by the unnecessary introduction of some abrupt phrase from common parlance. This is naturally more apparent in his earlier works: a conspicuous example of both of these faults is the great dying speech of Hallowes in " Smith." Ballads like " An Exodus from Houndsditch," or the " Vengeance of the Duchess," fail because their language is too commonplace for their thought; and, generally, Mr. Davidson is liable to lapse into the grotesque. Besides this, he is often led away by some fantastic simile, especially if he can haul in, head and shoulders, a reference to Nature.

Speaking generally, if one must find a purely technical fault in Mr. Davidson, that fault will be an impetuousness that leads him sometimes to disregard the symmetry and form of his work. He has too little restraint or power of self-criticism in matters purely artistic. Nevertheless, of his blank verse I will say simply that it is the best since that of Milton. Its majesty and grace cannot fail to impress all readers. It is packed and terse, like Marlowe's, varied, yet without Tennysonian thinness or the monotony of Shelley.

Perhaps the most interesting point about Mr. Davidson's poetry is his extraordinary objectivity. Mr. Davidson is the first realist that has appeared in English poetry. One is pleasantly surprised at that, as on first realizing that Milton was a Roundhead. Indeed, poetry has no greater foe than a gaudy veil of romance, which easily obscures the import of facts. And let me not forget to notice the extreme originality of the man. One or two of his earliest plays seem more or less influenced by the Elizabethans, but are so fresh and vivid that some of us would wish him to cast aside his purpose, and abandon himself once more to the Venus of pure delight. But there is little enough that resembles his eclogues, ballads, testaments, or plays; and we may still hope for a masterpiece greater than these; his work has, after all, only just begun. All Mr. Davidson's work is dramatic; the eclogues are so in form; the testaments are dramatic monologues; even the ballads breathe of drama. His most splendid dramatic achievement, "Self's the Man," is remarkable for extreme restraint and careful writing; it is not, like many plays in verse of to-day, a series of dialogues in decorated English. This "tragi-comedy" is quite stageable, full of incident, masterly in composition and form. The character of Urban, the tyrant-hero, is strongly drawn. In one fine scene, where Urban and his former mistress, Saturnia, meet in peril of their lives, we may experience that strange, almost physical thrill, that sense of the world being in harmony with the verse, which is only to be found here and there throughout literature, and which cannot be explained, save as a recollection of things experienced in a former existence. I have seen the "Cenci," called the best play since Shakespeare. A play in which one perpetually feels that the author is struggling to write lyrics cannot surely be compared with the "Duchess of Malfi." It is as certainly inferior to "Self's the Man."

The first work in which Mr. Davidson displays his characteristic attitude towards life is "Smith," the tragic farce, written in 1886. This play opens in a public-house. Brown, from Oxford, Jones, and Robinson are discussing the character of Hallowes, a poet. Brown, the very apostle of compromise, blames the poet for his absurd enthusiasms, and begins abusing Smith, who has a peculiar way of talking literature and philosophy with barmaids. Then Jones describes Smith as

> A mere savage, barbarous as a Lapp,
> A handsome creature, but elliptical.

In this triumvirate of fools, Brown is cultured and foolish, Jones epigrammatic and foolish, and Robinson, who has "points" to raise, and exclaims "fair, very fair" at intervals in sympathetic inanity, is fatuous and foolish; and they agree well together. Just as Brown has announced the fact that he is to wed his cousin Magdalen in a month, Smith bursts in upon them like a whirlwind. Smith is annoyed with their idle talk about Hallowes, and finally calls them

> The commonest type of biped crawling here.

And at length clears them out with

> You sots, you maggots, shavings, asteroids!
> A million of you wouldn't make a man!
> Out, or I'll strike you, monkeys, mannikins.

Hallowes enters and tells how he is going to his new-found retreat of Garth,

> In the North, a hamlet like a cave,
> Nestling unknown in tawny Merlin's side.

There, he says, he will write poetry, be it but one line a day. He rejects Smith's advice to "let fame alone"; Fame, says Hallowes, is the "breath of power," and he continues, clearly voicing the ideas of the dramatist himself:

> Give me to dream dreams all would love to dream;
> To tell the world's truth; hear the world tramp time
> With satin slippers and with hob-nailed shoes
> To my true singing: fame is worth its cost,
> Blood-sweats and tears, and haggard, homeless lives.
> How dare a man, appealing to the world,
> Content himself with ten! How dare a man
> Appeal to ten when all the world should hear!
> How dare a man conceive himself as else
> Than his own fool without the world's hurrah
> To echo him!
>   SMITH. But if the world won't shout
> Till he be dead?
>   HALLOWES. Let him address the street:
> No subtle essences, ethereal tones
> For senses sick, bed-ridden in the down
> Of culture and its stifling curtains.

They decide to go to Garth together, and Smith agrees with Hallowes in the last lines of the act:

You are right—one must become
Fanatic—be a wedge, a thunderbolt
To smite a passage through the close-grained world.

The next act introduces Graham, father of Magdalen, and Magdalen herself. With Magdalen, Smith falls in love at first sight, and in four pages of remarkable and splendid dialogue, he makes her confess that she is being made to marry Brown against her will, and that she finds in him, Smith, the masterful nature women love.

The passage contains the lines quoted above (p. 189)—

Think my thought, be impatient as I am.

The next scene takes place on the top of Mount Merlin where Hallowes is discovered lying with a note-book by his side. He has opened one of his veins, and is dying. After cursing his unhappiness and poverty, he speaks these glorious words, feeling death upon him:

But I have chosen Death. Death—and the moon
Hangs low and broad upon the eastern verge
Above a mist that floods the orient,
Filling the deep ravines and shallow vales,
Lake-like and wan, embossed with crested isles
Of pine and birch. Death—and the drops of day
Still stain the west a faintest tinge of rose
The stars cannot o'erwash with innocence.
Death—and the mountain tops, peak after peak,
Lie close and dark beneath Orion's sword.
Death—and the houses nestle at my feet,
With ruddy human windows here and there
Piercing the velvet shade—deep in the world,
Old hedge-rows and sweet by-paths through the corn!

The river like a sleepless eye looks up.
Pale shafts of smoke ascend from homely hearths,
And fade in middle air like happy sighs.
Death—and the wind blows chill across my face:
The thin, long, hoary grass waves at my side
With muffled tinkling. . . . Not yet! No; my life
Has not ebbed all away. I want to live
A little while. . . . Is the moon gone so soon?
They've put the shutters to, down there. . . The wind
Is warm. . . . Death—is it death? . . . I had no chance . . .
Perhaps I'll have another where I go. . . .
Another chance . . . How black! . . .   [*Dies.*

After this Smith is seen carrying Magdalen up to
the summit of the mountain, and the summit of their
own "mad happiness." While he is still standing,
amazed at the death of Hallowes, Graham and Brown
rush up in pursuit. A splendid scene follows. Smith
uses force to prevent them from taking Magdalen
from him. "Can we not go?" asks Magdalen. "Yes,"
Smith replies:

Yes, we can go where none will follow us.
We two could never love each other more
Than now we do; never our souls could mount
Higher on passion's fire-plumed wings; nor yet
Could laughter of our children's children pierce
With keener pangs of happiness our hearts.
I have a million things to tell my love,
But I will keep them for eternity.
Good earth, good mother earth, my mate and me—
Take us.
                [*He leaps with her over the precipice.* GRAHAM
                rushes forward, but falls fainting. Enter
                VILLAGERS, *shouting and laughing.*

I think enough has been said, enough extracts

given, to show that " Smith " brought something strong and vital into our literature.

All Mr. Davidson's work carries this same message of deliverance. Take the most powerful and the best written of his ballads, " The Ballad in Blank Verse of the Making of a Poet." It is a story told with intimate observation, and is perhaps drawn from experience. The scene is a Scottish port. A boy, whose romantic materialism seems to combine the types of Smith and Hallowes, is the source of all his parents' grief, because he refuses to acknowledge himself a Christian. When his parents talked to him of Christ he used to see

> The Cyprian Aphrodite, all one blush
> And glance of passion, from the violet sea
> Step inland, fastening as she went her zone.

His mother dies, heart-broken at his sinfulness. In a moment of weak contrition he takes the eucharist, and suddenly it crosses his mind,

> I eat and drink damnation to myself
> To give my Father's troubled spirit peace.

Yet there was no peace for the boy himself.

> But in the evening by the purple firth
> He walked and saw brown locks upon the brine,
> And pale hands beckon him to come away,
> Where Mermaids, with their harps and golden combs
> Sit throned upon the carven, antique poops
> Of treasure-ships, and soft sea-dirges sing
> Over the green-gilt bones of mariners.

He wanders on till night, pondering how all creeds

are one creed—the creed of slavery. Bidding them fly away like evil vultures, he is inspired by the idea that he is, after all, God to himself. That every man is his own God, has a right to will as he desires, he feels to be a doctrine of salvation, which he ought to proclaim to the world:

> At home, where millions mope, in labyrinths
> Of hideous streets astray without a clue,
> Unfed, unsexed, unsoulled, unhelped, I bring
> Life, with the Gospel—Up, quit you like Gods.

With this message he breaks in upon his father's new-found happiness, and plunges him in the bitterness of despair and sorrow.

> This was the sin of Lucifer
> To make himself God's equal.

And his father also dies of grief, crying out to his Saviour, wishing even to be sent to hell, if so he might see his boy again.

There follows a long passage of stately verse, wherein the boy, after cursing creed and dogma, proclaims the Gospel of "Self's the Man."

> I am a man set by to overhear
> The inner harmony, the very tune
> Of Nature's heart; to be a thoroughfare
> For all the pageantry of time; to catch
> The mutterings of the spirit and the hour
> And make them known; and of the lowliest
> To be the minister, and therefore reign
> Prince of the powers of the air, lord of the world
> And master of the sea. Within my heart
> I'll gather all the universe, and sing
> As sweetly as the spheres; and I shall be
> The first of men to understand himself. . . .

Nor can too high praise be given to the " Ballad of Heaven." Here a musician "toils at one great work for years." His wife and child die; he cannot feed or maintain them; he lives but for his music. Yet he is welcomed to Heaven by God himself, and by his wife and child:

> God, smiling, took him by the hand,
>   And led him to the brink of heaven:
> He saw where systems whirling stand,
>   Where galaxies like snow are driven.
>
> Dead silence reigned; a shudder ran
>   Through space : Time furled his weared wings ;
> A slow adagio then began,
>   Sweetly resolving troubled things.
>
> The dead were heralded along ;
>   As if with drums and trumps of flame
> And flutes and oboes keen and strong
>   A brave andante singing came.
>
> Then, like a python's sumptuous dress
>   The frame of things was cast away,
> And, out of Time's obscure distress
>   The conquering scherzo thundered Day.
>
> He doubted ; but God said, " Even so ;
>   Nothing is lost that 's wrought with tears.
> The music that you made below
>   Is now the music of the spheres.

Of the other ballads, many of them, as also the " Ordeal," treat of that fine type of woman which Mr. Davidson has created for himself—a woman strong in her loves and hates, fit wife of a strong man —a woman of the force of Agrippina without her malignant cruelty—a woman naturally queen. Be-

sides these, I will only mention the fine ballad of
Tannhäuser. Mr. Davidson gives the tale a different
ending from what we know best. In it Tannhäuser
returns to his first mistress in the Venusberg, having
been rejected by the Pope, and lives with her in
immortal happiness :

> As he lay worshipping his bride
>   While rose-leaves in her bosom fell,
> And dreams came sailing on a tide
>   Of sleep, he heard a matin-bell.
>
> "Hark, let us leave the magic hill,"
>   He said, "and live on earth with men."
> "No ; here," she said, " we stay until
>   The golden age shall come again."
>
> And so they wait, while empires sprung
>   Of hatred thunder past above,
> Deep in the earth, for ever young,
>   Tannhäuser, and the Queen of love.

Mr. Davidson adds an interesting note, as follows:

The story of Tannhäuser is best known in the sophisticated
version of Wagner's great opera. In reverting to a simpler form
I have endeavoured to present passion rather than sentiment,
and once more to bear a hand in laying the ghost of an un-
wholesome idea that still haunts the world—the idea of the
inherent impurity of Nature. I beg to submit to those who may
be disposed to think with me, and also those who, though otherwise minded, are at liberty to alter their opinions, that "A new
Ballad of Tannhäuser" is not only the most modern, but the
most humane interpretation of the world-legend with which it
deals.

We now come to the "Testaments." The first is
the amazing "Testament of a Vivisector," which

neither upholds nor reprobates vivisection. The vivisector vivisects himself. Mr. Davidson indeed has been praised for condemning vivisection, for is not vivisection "an infamy too gross for the common terms of scorn, contempt, and abhorrence?" but we shall see that we have only to read the author's prefatory note to find that any such view is false.

The "Testament of a Vivisector" is the first of a series of Poems I propose publishing at intervals in this form . . . and the new statement of Materialism it contains is likely to offend both the religious and the irreligious mind. This poem, therefore, and its successors, my Testaments, are addressed to those who are willing to place all ideas in the crucible, and who are not afraid to fathom what is subconscious in themselves and others.

"The Testament of a Vivisector" to many will appear repulsive, for the vivisector proclaims and brazens out the fact that he loves vivisection because it fills him with a pleasing sense of mastery, and because it satisfies his lust for inflicting pain. Few things more grimly straightforward have been written. Anyone reading it will appreciate the title, "John Davidson, Realist." In the "Testament of a Man Forbid" we have Smith once more, struggling against an unsympathetic world, exclaiming against the men

That balance libraries upon their polls.

The exordium is superb.

"The Testament of an Empire-Builder" opens humorously after the old fashion of "Scaramouch.' The Empire-Builder has a vision of the beasts, who are talking about man. They discuss his infirmities, his selfishness, his power. Nennook the Polar Bear explains to the Mastiff that he is unhappy about his prospects of immortality, and of the endless heavenly feast

> On blubbered seals that slumber on the floes.

In reply,

> A flea, ensconced behind the Mastiff's ear,
> Chirruped aloud, " Nennook, my friend, take heart :
> I, for example, must be soundly squelched,
> But the idea of the flea remains ;
> For race continues always : permanence
> Of species is established theory.

> " Established Nonsense, neighbour ; hold your tongue,"
> Snorted the domineering Elephant,

who goes on to catalogue extinct species of beasts— the mammoth, the plesiosaur, and so on. A bumptious groundling ape is informed that man would exterminate him if he had any sense. The hackney and the lion also detail their woes, and the skunk makes occasional interpolations by way of comic relief. The nightmare over, the Empire-Builder discovers himself in an English lane, watching Butcher-birds with interest and admiration. The rest of the Testament contains quite a novel idea, that is also worked out in the " Prime Minister," namely, that the proud in spirit are quartered in heaven, while the poor in spirit are dismissed to hell. Mr. Davidson's whole doctrine seems to me to lie in the title of his play—" Self's the Man." He goes even further than Ibsen, as he has himself hinted in the preface to "Godfrida." Ibsen's message was "Break conventions if they hinder true happiness or noble action." He has perhaps blurred the outline of his doctrine by his natural mysticism—strange voices of earth and air that call Brand as he dies amid the avalanche of his broken ideals. Those people who will be apt to say that Mr. Davidson's rationalism is now out of date, and who continue to acquiesce in what they know to be a palpable lie, will probably think that the message "Break convention" is an old one, now obsolete. To such people unconventionality seems to mean little more than wearing a cap on Sunday. It was no freakish foolery that Ibsen commended; his message was as fresh as dawn. He urged the overhauling of all our social machinery; he attacked with terrible precision the shoddy idealism and the prudish self-complacency that still pervades modern life. How can Mr. Davidson go even further than this? It is in this way. He says not only "Break conventions that stand in your way," but "live as if convention, as if Christianity, as if thirty centuries of literature had never existed." He puts a new and far more difficult interpretation on the "Know thyself" of old. To this his doctrine, he assigns as metaphysic not mysticism, but materialism.

Intimately connected with Mr. Davidson's philosophy of life is his passion for the country. He loves Nature for her simplicity and beauty, and writes about it as if it were a new and particular revelation, as if it had never become a hackneyed theme, as if Spring-Poets had never been by-words. We have seen how it is sometimes a hindrance. He can never turn his thoughts away from the fields for long. As for the sea, what could be more convincing than these lines from the " Man Forbid "?

> The bosomed plain
> That strips her green robe to the saffron shore,
> And steps into the surf, where threads and scales
> And arabesques of blue and emerald wave
> Begin to damascene the iron sea.

I doubt if the most ardent admirer would stand by this Reformer in his utter condemnation of Christianity, convention, and culture, and take refuge in a Materialism that says the body and soul are one. But more might be inclined to agree with the fascinating theory held unconsciously by the Greeks, and held very consciously by this least Greek of poets—the theory of Man's natural sinlessness. If Calvary has a meaning for Mr. Davidson, it means the death of sin. Many again would strenuously deny that culture is evil, claiming perhaps that nothing leads a man to Reality, to the examination of Self and of Conventions, to a broad and catholic view of life, with more inevitable sureness than a liberal education, and the tolerance that only culture can instil. Yet have we not all been at times disgusted by the men that display an apathy proportionate to their learning? Do we not know and hate the type of individual that takes Holy Orders out of a vague desire to improve humanity by his miserable assistance—that is, by preaching a creed which he neither firmly believes nor thoroughly understands? Do not the courts of the temple swarm with those who fear to commit themselves to anything in heaven above or earth beneath? I have observed it is with this apathy that Mr. Davidson has had to contend. For twenty years he has been preaching a sermon of great meaning, and he has received nothing but compliments on his poetical "cornucopia." No wonder he finds little consolation in culture, as he writes Play, Ballad, Eclogue, and Testament, repeating his tremendous tale with magnificent variety.   There is a hard lesson for us in the writings of Mr. Davidson. We are convinced by him that if we want to found our idealism on some basis less flimsy than that of sentiment, we must strip off the ideals that now obsess us. If we desire to arrive at a true appreciation of life or literature, we must criticize as if no one had anticipated us in the work.   To compensate for nineteen hundred years of error, we must cultivate the neglected virtue of strength. Only thus can we be ourselves, and fully realize our latent power.

After all, the thesis of Materialism that we find set before us here is not so repellent as it seems. After years of what is little better than Manicheeism we are at last told that Matter is not impure but lovely; that man should be "one with the mountains"; that the landscapes of the world are beautiful, not because of a soul residing in them, nor because their creator had aesthetic ideals, but because they are what they are— lovely in themselves.

JOHN DAVIDSON

I

I HAVE only had the privilege of talking to one great poet in my life, and that was John Davidson. He was somewhat like one of his own ballads in appearance; fiery, impenitent, yet subdued to convention —the eye-glass seeming to assert a right to aristocracy, the well-trimmed imperial hinting at eccentric elegance. He was in all ways a self-confident, ostentatious man. His egoism showed in his handwriting, which sloped upwards to the right across the page at a terrific angle. It shows in almost every line of his poetry, in the very audacity and splendour of his image:

> And out of Time's obscure distress
> The conquering Scherzo thundered day.

His poetry, unjustly neglected as it is, does not require very detailed criticism. He was, after all, the greatest poet of his age; but it was not a glorious age. Poetry was dead. Swinburne had written the immortal " Ave Atque Vale," and somehow therewith had sung hail and farewell to his own inspiration and the splendid Victorian Muse.

The names and traditions of the Victorian epoch should be banished as ἄρρητα—things too holy (or unholy) to be spoken—from the pages of a journal which encourages young British poets. After forty years those gigantic shadows still oppress us. I must trust entirely to my memory, but I believe that in twenty years' interval were published, "The House of Life," "Omar Khayyám," "The Scholar Gipsy," "Dramatic Lyrics," "The Princess," and "Atalanta in Calydon," any one of which masterpieces, even the "Princess," would have dominated the whole succeeding period from their age to ours. In those days William Morris and Christina Rossetti were minor poets. For all the imperishable work done since their time by Housman and by Yeats, by Kipling and by John Davidson himself, for all the progress in artistic taste made by our younger generation, who at least never write such vulgar rubbish as "Locksley Hall," nor such obscure rubbish as "Pachiarotto," we know that English poetry is awaiting another dawn, and that we poets of to-day are but torch-bearers in a twilight.

John Davidson realized, I think, for all his mask of aggressive self-confidence, that his poetry, judged by the hard standard of his immediate predecessors, was a failure; and it embittered him. But it is only when measured by that hard standard that his poetry fails. The world will always read those virile and impetuous ballads. They have a cadence of bronze, and their effects are those of a rhetoric which imagination and sometimes insolence has transmuted into poetry. Charming as are his "Fleet Street Eclogues," and also some of his short lyrics, the ballads are his great achievement. He might have added to them, for they are but few, collected them, pruned them of many harsh or feeble expressions. But he suddenly lost all interest in his lyric work; the peculiar curse of the British author had fallen upon him. He discovered the secret of the Universe, and he felt a call to make the discovery universal. He began to preach, and to preach in blank verse; and he abused the critics who preferred what he now called the tinkle of his rhyme to what he thought was the important splendour of his new metre.

John Davidson was a man of great genius, but of still greater ambition. His ambition ruined his genius, and his preachings in blank verse, despite their gorgeous imagery, even despite occasional humour and originality, are failures. They fail owing to the crudeness of the poetical ideas and the technical inferiority of the verse.

Tennyson, and in later years Mr. Stephen Phillips in " Marpessa," and Mr. Yeats, have cleverly turned blank verse to purely lyrical uses. Swinburne, with his rows of monosyllables, gave his blank verse a heavy beat, which was a fine device when his inspiration soared, and an intolerable trick when it flagged. But the last master of blank verse was Browning. All through the interminable meanderings of " The Ring and the Book," the technical excellence of the blank verse never fails, and at its greatest can be measured with Shakespeare's only.

To get at the reason of success or failure in blank verse is the hardest task of criticism. Take the fol-

lowing lines from the "Testament of John Davidson":

> At sunset on the mountain of my choice
> I stood above the catafalque of day
> And watched the quilted vapours harness heaven
> And chrysolite and ruby of countless hues,
> Unnamed, unknown, unthought of, only guessed
> Upon the moment of vicissitude
> And pulsing cadence; while the lofty winds'
> Unseen battalions swung their shining glaives
> Against me, and across the hills behind
> With bridle-bells apeal and vibrant tread
> Went down into the gloaming and the night.

This is all very magnificent, and somehow not worth
any three lines of Browning you can set your
eyes on:

>   Some interchange
> Of grace, some splendour once the very thought,
> Some benediction anciently they smile.

These "chrysolites and rubies," these "unseen battalions," could pass off well enough in rhyme. Insert
any nonsense:

> The lofty winds were striding through the waves:
> Unseen battalions swung their shining glaives
> Against me, and across the hills behind
> With pulsing cadence a more lofty wind
> With bridle-bells apeal and vibrant tread
> Went down into the gloaming and the dead.

How much happier are the fine phrases with the
discipline of rhyme, however foolish, to add to their
elegance and excuse their bravado! For rhyme, in its

subtle way, gives them, or at least the final word of them, a reason for existence.

Blank verse, to repeat old truisms, must be written not only as carefully as rhymed verse, but must aim at a quite different impression. It must be written in paragraphs, and not for the effect of single lines. John Davidson sins, I think, even against these old and obvious rules: yet there is something deeper than their strict observance needed to enable even the good poet to make good blank verse. I think of Shakespeare, Webster, Milton, as well as Browning, when I say that it is something like a latent but ever-watchful sense of humour.

Meanwhile, even as a man's character is laid bare in his cups, so a poet's intellect is betrayed by his blank verse. John Davidson was a well-read, but not a well-educated man. He felt an imperious desire to assert himself, and began to preach in his new blank verse with prose prefaces, a crude egoism and a peculiarly childish materialism. The disaster is, of course, not that he should have believed this or that. A great poet may be a crude Catholic like Crashaw, or a crude Protestant like Milton. The disaster is that John Davidson bores us with his beliefs, having nothing but a lot of rhetoric about "passionate molecules and atomic pairs" to cover up its bare and very ugly skeleton. These latter works are no longer of John Davidson the poet, but of John Davidson from Perth in Scotland.

II

Almost all the chief poets of the last hundred years have been comparatively rich men, or at least have not been forced to struggle bitterly for a bare existence. Byron, Shelley, Tennyson, Matthew Arnold, Browning, Swinburne, were all men in fairly easy circumstances. When there has been misery and poverty in the lives of poets—of Coleridge and Keats, for example—it has usually had an effect adverse to their genius. This generalization could be tested in other climes and other times, and would, I believe, admit few exceptions; nor can I think of any poets, save Villon and Verlaine, who drew directly inspiration from the distress of a vagabond existence.

Yet the public still excuses itself from its obvious duty towards poets by hypocrisies concerning the beneficial effect of the struggle for life. When the struggle for life is almost over, and the poetic inspiration has been worn away by misery, the unfortunate genius is sometimes accorded as an alms, and not as an honour, a pension about equal to a footman's wage.

One of the meanest tragedies in the history of English literature was the life and death of John Davidson. He bore heroically the most abject poverty. And the pity of it is that one is convinced that, had he been enabled since the days when he published his first plays—so full of life and promise —to lead an ordinary decent life of ease and comfort, perhaps to travel and air his genius in a wider world, he might have become a far greater poet and might have dominated his age for the advantage of English letters. He would have lost that rude savagery of nature which made him rant materialism like a Hyde Park missionary.

As it happened, his pension, such as it was, came too late. I think he felt, too, that his muse was dead He imagined, rightly or wrongly, that his health was undermined. He had been a brave man all his life, and he was brave enough to commit suicide. As his body could not at first be found, the British public heard, for the first time, from their newspapers, that there was a poet called John Davidson.

And so the world goes on, and millionaires leave their millions to found public libraries to be filled with the books that men wrote, and are writing still, in misery, untended sickness, or at best in hours stolen from uncongenial toil—books, too, which would have been more bravely penned were great writers able now to live, as they lived in Rome or Greece, like gentlemen. When such vast funds are instantly subscribed not only by millionaires for libraries, but by the most generous and most thoughtless public in the world, for any specious and delusive charity the daily papers choose to encourage, cannot a few thousands be collected to publish the books, if not to prolong the lives, of those who, like John Davidson, write not for ten thousand to read in ten days, but for ten more wise men to read every year for ever?

THE NEW POETRY AND MR. HOUS-
MAN'S "SHROPSHIRE LAD"

THE man who treats poetry as a scholar treats his classics, with loving care and affectionate reverence, the man who loves the muse Euterpe because she is so beautiful, and not because she is the sister of Clio or the handmaid of Urania, will ever continue to judge of poetry line by line and poem by poem, judging by the only true and just standard. He will, perhaps, never realize the attitude of that outer circle of readers, those veritable amateurs who, loving Poetry less intelligently but no less sincerely than himself, yet are not content with vivid fancies, delicate thoughts, and sweet expressions and powerful harmonies, but seek in what they read for a statement of philosophy, or at least a uniform and attractive view of the World, Life and Love. Thus it is so many Englishmen consider that Poetry died with Tennyson or lives only with Swinburne. Modern poetry appears to be in so chaotic a state that it is impossible to trace any definite new movement, or the prevalence of any distinctive new idea. Unable to discover a main tendency, a predominating idea in contemporary verse, many condemn the whole as minor, and complain that Poetry is dead.

While it is intended to show here that there is a main movement, a real tendency in modern poetry, it is merely to revive a flagging interest. Poetry becomes no better by being made a part of a movement. It must, of course, be taken on its merits line by line and poem by poem. But it may become more interesting. It is our object here to show that the significance and trend of modern poetry is the creation of a new poetical language to supersede the Victorian convention.

Poetry is not dead, but the older generation is right in saying that the Older Poetry is dead. The famous English Poets from Coleridge to Swinburne form a strong, a splendid, a connected dynasty, only once interrupted, and that for only a decade. These men bear a strong resemblance to each other in the vigour of their thought, in the dignity of their style, and, one may add, in the portentous volume of their works. Even Shelley, untimely cut off at the age of thirty, has left more work than a thousand large pages— more than forty thousand lines of verse, more than all we possess of Lucretius, Virgil, Horace, and Propertius. This amazing fertility was undoubtedly a sign of strength and health, of an activity parallel to that of the Elizabethan age, and founded in the same way on a sense of national greatness. But the sense of the dignity of the Muses, of the importance of some more or less vague personal mission, was far more prominent in these men than it had been among the humbler writers of our drama. The great Victorian poets clearly felt their own importance.

Wordsworth and Browning were philosophers, Byron, Shelley, and Swinburne revolutionaries, Rossetti and Morris were the leaders of an enthusiastic brother-hood, Coleridge and Matthew Arnold employed themselves in criticism. Even Keats worked very consciously for his ideal of Beauty, and the official position of Tennyson dignified the pronouncements of " In Memoriam." It was natural, however, that these merits should bring corresponding defects. The moral and philosophic tone of the Victorians sometimes destroyed their inspiration; and the enormous bulk of their volumes was bound to contain a rather unnecessary proportion of " poems with a purely biographical interest." Matthew Arnold, for instance, may seem to some to have obtained by means of his prose writings, and by means of rather tangible and obvious poetic effects, an unmerited popularity for his verses, the melody of which is often harsh and the sentiment civilian. But even he keeps his place by four or five magnificent poems, and in the end we are compelled to admit, not only that all these poets deserve their high reputations, but also that in grandeur of diction no modern or new author has approached the best work of these epic song-writers.

They are still flattered by imitation and before coming to what is significant, we may well dismiss what is insignificant in modern poetry. In America especially, a country that still looks upon Macaulay as the typical English prose writer, there has been no attempt to follow the tradition of Whitman and write *American* instead of English. America approves of poets who write the now foreign language of the British Isles, and the result is that her most popular versifiers can do nothing but imitate Tennyson; never realizing that there is as much chance of immortality for these experiments in an unknown tongue as there was for the Latin poems written by the learned Italians of the late Renaissance.

The English living imitators of Victorian style also claim a moment's notice. Of these Mr. Stephen Phillips is the most important. The grave sonority of " Christ in Hades," the pleasant metrical variation of " Marpessa " produced a certain impression. That " Marpessa " is a *tour de force* is obvious upon close analysis; that Mr. Stephen Phillips is a close follower and rather slavish imitator of Tennyson can be proved. And if that vulgar phrase of the journalists, " clever but uninspired," can be employed justly of anyone, it can be employed of those plays, so successful on the stage, whose rather meretricious wonders impressed the London mob.

Mr. William Watson, a writer far duller and less skilful than Mr. Phillips, has tried in a most brazen manner to re-write Keats, Tennyson, and even Stevenson—(he begins a poem: " Under the dark and piny steep "). The temporary reputation acquired by Mr. Watson is particularly pernicious to the well-being of Poetry; and it is ridiculous as well as aggravating that any notice should be taken of his pompous outcries.

The poetical language imitated by these writers, that of the nineteenth century, is in obvious distinction to that of the eighteenth. Blake, the André Chénier of English Romanticism, drew upon the Elizabethans and the inspiration of divine ecstasy to replenish his idiom. Coleridge turned to the old ballads, and Wordsworth to Nature and the rustics. But there was nothing rustic in the convention that they formed—a convention admirably suited for the expression of the high ideals and fervid thoughts of themselves and their successors. The royal harmonies of Hyperion, the voluptuously falling cadences of Rossetti, the clear rustle of Tennyson's measure, the impetuosity of Shelley and Swinburne, spring from a nearly identical convention, rich and infinitely variable, which nevertheless yearly became more distant from the general language of mankind. In all the manners really congenial to them the style, and usually the theme, of Swinburne and Tennyson is classical.

Meanwhile, concurrent with this lofty literature, a popular style of Poetry never ceased to exist, a poetry where popular idiom was permitted, and popular subjects allowed. The greater poets attempted this frequently, and Rossetti's " Jenny " is a fine example of a style he too seldom employed; but the real masters of this more secular verse were the prose writers, Charles Lamb and Thackeray, and the poets, Hood and Patmore. A word must be said of Browning in this connection. He made a desperate and conscious effort to introduce the language of conversation into his poetry, but he fell into a mistake into which Mr. Kipling sometimes falls—that of using

slang and more or less vulgar language by preference.

Swinburne again, in the "Sisters," has made a weird
and disastrous effort to use plain speech. In his other
plays he uses the phraseology of conversation either
by contrast or else to obtain weighty monosyllabic
lines of blank verse, and thereby to lay a heightened
and unnatural stress on the single words. Shelley's
"Cenci" is an earlier and perhaps more successful
attempt in the same style. But the most signal
example of a conscious combination of what may be
briefly called "old and new" comes from Tennyson.
The exquisite poem to Fitzgerald, beginning

> Old Fitz who from your suburb grange

is not only simpler and more sincere, but also in a far
more natural vein than the bulk of his work, and,
more especially still, it contains a pathetic parody of
his own usual splendid verbiage. The poem of
"Tiresias" found

> With shallow scraps of manuscript
> And dating many a year ago

is enclosed between two addresses to Fitzgerald, one
written to the living, the other to the dead. Quoting
from the last lines of "Tiresias" right into the second
poem

> while the golden lyre
> Is ever sounding in heroic ears
> Heroic hymns, and every way the vales
> Wind, clouded with the grateful incense-fume
> Of those who mix all odour to the gods
> On one far height in one far-shining fire.

"One height and one far-shining fire,"
    And while I fancied that my friend
For this brief idyll would require
    A less diffuse and opulent end

And would defend his judgment well
    If I should deem it over nice,
The tolling of his funeral bell
    Broke on my pagan Paradise.

For Tennyson in his old age this, and not that of
"In Memoriam," was the language of sincerity and
sorrow.

The work of yet another poet can afford a striking
contrast of this sort. In the "Sphinx" Oscar Wilde
compressed and exaggerated the sumptuous glories
of the old style by the aid of a vast vocabulary drawn
from the storehouse of French romanticism:

And did you mark the Cyprian kiss
White Adon on his catafalque,
And did you follow Amanalk
The God of Heliopolis?
And did you talk with Thoth, and did
You hear the moon-horned Io weep,
And know the painted Kings who sleep
Beneath the wedge-shaped pyramid?

Withal the "Sphinx" is a vigorous and lively poem.
Words are used for the sheer joy of their sonorous
eccentricity, and the wild rhetoric gives the effect of
a gorgeous nightmare. Two years before, he wrote of
a prisoner in his poem, "The Ballad of Reading Gaol":

He walked among the trial men
In a suit of shabby grey;

> A cricket cap was on his head
> And his step seemed light and gay,
> But I never saw a man who looked
> So wistfully at the day.

Now this is the language of almost all that is best in modern poetry. It was by no means Wilde's invention: "Reading Gaol" is later than John Davidson's ballads, and later than the "Shropshire Lad." It is the language of Bridges, Hardy, and Yeats, and of all the significant writers that are younger still. But of all volumes of modern verse the "Shropshire Lad" is the most complete vindication of this new and simple style, and is therefore a fit example to be given here.

Mr. A. E. Housman is famous as a classical scholar. This fact, and the fact that among these loving descriptions of English country life and manners we find a classical manner and view of life, or even a classical theme, make it all the more surprising that he should have so entirely broken away from the tradition that gave us Tennyson's "Ulysses," Swinburne's "Erechtheus," or Mr. Murray's Swinburnian translations of "Euripides." It is curious and pleasant to find interspersed among these village songs stray memories of the distant past of a distant land:

> A Grecian lad, as I hear tell,
> One that many loved in vain,
> Looked into a forest well
> And never looked away again.
> There when the turf in spring-time flowers,
> With downward eye and gazes sad
> Stands amid the glancing showers
> A jonquil, not a Grecian lad.

This poem is marked by no difference of style from
the others; and no one can fail to recognize here as
elsewhere a happy exactness, a delight in making the
point that, apart from any reference to the subject,
mark the scholar. We are reminded of Landor at his
briefest and best. Another poem, called "The Merry
Guide," describes how a youth with mien to match the
morning, a youth with friendly brows, led the poet
across glittering pastures, and by hanging woods, and
by silver waters to the music of the great gale. The
guide is some mysterious stranger, we know not who:
the secret, preciously hidden for so long, is in the last
verse wonderfully revealed :

> And midst the fluttering legion
>   Of all that ever died
> I follow and before us
>   Goes the delightful guide,
> With lips that brim with laughter
>   But never once respond,
> And feet that fly on feathers,
>   And serpent-circled wand.

We have begun by dwelling on an aspect of this
work which, though fascinating, is not of paramount
importance. At all events, the extracts serve as an
introduction to anything there may be to say on the
metres of the "Shropshire Lad." Except by Mr.
Davidson in his powerful tales in verse, the simple
stanzas of the ballads have not been often successfully
used in the nineteenth century. In this book there
are no complicated or involved measures, and no blank
verse. There is one metre, however, the structure of
which calls for especial notice.

> Here of a Sunday morning
>   My love and I would lie,
> And see the coloured counties,
>   And hear the lark so high
>   About us in the sky.

It is a charming metre: the scazonic effect of the last line is wistfully harmonious. I would not rashly call it new. Who can lightly glance over all English Poetry with its manifold wealth of form to resolve such a question? But doubtless the author invented it for himself, and it is a fine invention, or, at all events, a fine resuscitation.

There is also a simple metre rhyming in couplets, which the poet uses to obtain a majestic grace rather foreign to the quiet compassion, or compassionate horror, of the rest of the book:

> The flag of morn in conqueror's state
> Enters at the English gate ;
> The vanquished Eve, as night prevails
> Bleeds upon the road to Wales.

We may compare with these powerful lines the elaborate and sumptuous metaphor in the first verse of "Reveille," which is in the older style:

> Wake: the silver dusk returning
>   Up the beach of darkness brims,
> And the ship of sunrise, burning,
>   Strands upon the Eastern rims.

Within metres almost as limited and simple as those employed with ascetic choice by the author of "Emaux et Camées," Mr. Housman exhibits a great subtlety of workmanship. It would not only be dreadfully

prosaic, but also rather unfair to expose at any length
his wizard tricks. The infinite joys that all true lovers
of poetry find in the deft manipulation of verbal
sounds are almost too sacred for explanation. Let a
short poem be quoted almost at random:

> Now hollow fires burn out to black,
>   And lights are guttering low.
> Square your shoulders, lift your pack,
>   And leave your friends, and go.
>
> O never fear, man: nought's to dread,
>   Look not left nor right.
> In all the endless road you tread
>   There's nothing but the night.

The quiet and forcible alliterations of the first and last
lines, the surprising vigour of the third, the impressive
slowness of the fifth line is remarkable. There is,
moreover, an art in the juxtaposition of sounds about
which it is rather sacrilegious to talk, not because of
any superhuman merit in this particular poem, but
because the art of melody is one of suggestion, and
not of code. For we must not overpraise Mr. Housman.
As an inventive author we neither need nor dare compare him with the great names of the past. The verse
of Mr. Bridges[1] shows only too well by its combination
of impeccable technique and extreme dullness and
dearth of ideas, that it is all too easy to make lines
sound pleasant in English by using simple language
and simple metres. Spoken English is so intrinsically
beautiful that a phrase like

> Look not left nor right

---

[1] In later life Flecker became enthusiastic about Mr. Bridges.

goes straight into poetry. Thus the very medium employed saves writers who employ the simpler style from those lapses into weakness or ugliness that beset the Victorians. It is far easier to preserve the virtues of terseness and strength in short and simple lines than in long and involved metres. A quiet style could never perpetrate such a line as that

> Who prop, thou ask'st, in these bad days my mind?

which Matthew Arnold permitted to remain through edition after edition of his works at the head of a fine sonnet. It is of course true that verse which is technically easy to construct is liable to lapse into carelessness of substance and idea: and the "Shropshire Lad" is not free from weak and sentimental poems, from poems where the military subject is left to itself, as it were, to create an impression of strength, and others that express a mood and a thought so fleeting as to be without value. But, and this could be said of few books of vigorous poetry, there are no cacophonous lines.

Mr. Housman has achieved this fine result mainly because he has used pure spoken English with hardly any admixture of poetic verbiage. Indeed, some may blame him for putting such pleasant phrases into the mouths of peasants. If Browning was to be blamed for making his nobles talk slang, shall we not blame the poet who makes his peasants talk English?

While Mr. Housman's real justification for this is the great superiority of artistic effect, it is nevertheless a serious mistake to imagine that all peasants talk a coarse and corrupt tongue. Certainly in some parts of England a dialect is spoken which is fit only for caricature. But in other parts, such as the Welsh Borderlands, the natives speak in marvellously pure English. Similarly, Mr. Hardy's peasants talk at times the most excellent English, and a similar charge of unreality has been brought against them. Mr. Hardy seems to attempt some defence for this, when, at the beginning of " Tess," he explains the refined speech of his heroine by a reference to the fourth standard of the Board School. It is a prosaic, but probable explanation. At all events Mr. Housman can by no means be said always to transcribe the peasant speech. It is his to invent, not to copy, and he makes subtle alterations which affect the poetry without changing the general impression of simplicity. The poem on Bredon Hill, of which a verse has just been quoted above, is put into the mouth of a peasant lover. He might possibly have talked of " coloured counties," or used some very similar phrase. But no lover would have said the lark was " about" him in the sky. He would have said "above" undoubtedly. The change gives strength to the metre, and vigour to the phrase; but it is thoroughly artificial.

But it is not the subtlety of its language but its unity of subject, and its charm of feeling that has made the " Shropshire Lad" almost a famous book, and enabled it to weather indifference. There is something even Homeric in his treatment of the old themes, Love, War, and Death, in a simple and young community. His lovers affect no higher idealism, no trappings of middle-class sentiment. The sense of the bloom fading from the rose, of the close following of Death upon Love is the note of the Greek Anthology:

> Lovers lying two and two
> Ask not whom they sleep beside,
> And the bridegroom all night through
> Never turns him to the bride.

Moreover, lest we get any idea of some foolish Arcadia where pine the lovesick swains, there are poems on suicide, murder, and " men that tread on air." For better or for worse fierce sins and a ghastly retribution are features of all English village life:

> And naked to the hangman's noose
> The morning clocks will ring
> A neck God made for other use
> Than strangling in a string.
>   .   .   .
> So here I'll watch the night and wait
> To see the morning shine,
> When he will hear the stroke of eight,
> And not the stroke of nine.

The whole poem is very terrible: and then in the next we are back again   .   .   .   .   .   .

[*Here this early unpublished essay breaks off.*]

TWO CRITICS OF POETRY

"History of English Poetry." By W. J. Courthope. Vol. VI. London: Macmillan and Co. 10s. net.

"The Romantic Movement in English Poetry." By Arthur Symons. London: Constable and Co. 7s. 6d. net.

DURING the last year two histories of the Byronic period of English poetry have been laid before a public which prefers the criticism of poetry to poetry itself: one of these is by Mr. Courthope, a professor, the other by Mr. Symons, a poet. Both books are notable in their way; but their ways are different.

For the professor, poetry is one side of the History of England, every poet the mouthpiece of his age. He views all romantic literature as a phase of the party struggle between Whig and Tory, a struggle enlivened by a third element, that passionate adoration of Liberty, that unworldly determination to wreck the social order, and to build the New Jerusalem in the pleasant fields of England. That so wild a temper as this last is repellent to Mr. Courthope his attitude clearly shows, though he strives hard to conceal his repulsion. Yet however foolish politically, this idea directly inspired all the great poetry of the age, save that of Crabbe and Keats.

Mr. Courthope's method of criticism is imperial, almost brutal. He estimates poets by their influence rather than by their merit; this is excusable; but to estimate their merit by their influence, to allow direct literary criticism to be coloured by the contemporary importance or posthumous popularity of the poet, is not excusable. But Mr. Courthope does this. Fascinated by the great personality and power of Byron, he bestows exaggerated praise on those lyrical dramas whose bombast, tumidity, and conceit Meredith's curt sonnet has immortally damned. Yet even Mr. Courthope can find little to say in their defence save that they are good, sound English and tolerable blank verse. Again, we may forgive our author for reviving some names, that of Mason, for instance, for their political rather than their poetical importance. But can we forgive him for writing pages on Hogg without mentioning Kilmenie or the fairies? Can we forgive him for entirely omitting Darley, Jane and Ann Taylor, and a score of other interesting names in a book which styles itself a History of English Poetry, in a volume full of Southey, Erasmus Darwin, and the Della Cruscans? Or for perpetuating that old and vicious sophistry that we cannot estimate the value of poetry till the writers thereof are soundly dead, and there is some trend of a muddy popular opinion for a critic to seize hold of, and for being frightened, in accordance with this fear, of giving us any estimate of those rising young poets of to-day—Tennyson, Browning, and Rossetti?

But, after all, Professor Courthope is an enthusiast. When he finds any verse which he considers patriotic and healthy, such as Campbell's tinsel "Battle of the Baltic"—a rather mean poem for a rather mean occasion —or Scott's boyish, charming, quite unimportant Ballads, he indulges in extravagant applause. When he is writing of Blake and Keats we feel that for him they are simply a pair of conceited asses with a spark of genius; we know that had Mr. Courthope been on the "Edinburgh" at the time he would have had no good to say of such miserable poetasters. Blake—this seems to be the half-conscious trend of professorial thought—Blake had no interest or influence in politics or society: he was a mystic; mysticism is nonsense, and Blake a conceited ass. Keats, again, was no gentleman; his vulgarity occasionally appears in his verse (this, of course, is true, and Mr. Courthope fairly gloats over it); he was sensual, not in Byron's flashy patrician way, but with all the real viciousness of the lower middle-classes; his heroes are swooning fellows, not healthy Britons; a passage in "Lamia" is too disgusting for quotation; Keats had no interest in politics; Keats was a conceited ass. Most modern poets have followed Keats' devotion to his art and appealed to a circle of cultured admirers. They, too, are conceited asses.

Mr. Arthur Symons, on the other hand, prefers poetry to politics; and his book, though neither great criticism nor great literature, is superior to that of Mr. Courthope both in matter and in manner. Mr. Symons is himself something of a poet; it is too often forgotten that though artists may be very bad critics, they are the only people really fit to criticize. It must be admitted, however, that the appreciation of an art by a critic who practises himself is apt to be intense, but narrow. So with Mr. Symons. For instance, he starts by defining poetry as everything written in metre. This is the common-sense definition; it is the only definition: it is amazing that no one seems to have thought of it before. But while Mr. Symons has a fine talent for understanding and judging Romantics and Realists, he takes the bigoted view of Keats with regard to the Augustan Age of English verse. (By the way, Mr. Courthope thinks Keats an exceptionally conceited ass for abusing so distinguished a man as Boileau. He should read Landor on the absurdities of that dismal Frenchman.) In consequence Mr. Symons has no good to say of Pope. If Pope is poetry, he declares, then neither Elizabethan nor Romantic verse is poetry at all. He thus falls into the old error of using poetry in the sense of good, Romantic, or inspired verse; and into the more serious error of failing to see that Pope is great literature in verse, and therefore a great poet, according to his own definition. Mr. Symons does not perhaps see that the devotion to Pope which so many profess nowadays is essentially romantic. If he could feel any sympathy for the elegance and wit of the age of which Pope was so striking a representative, he might begin to feel the force and humanity of his verse. The emotions that poetry should inspire need not surely be all elevated or elemental. Are lyrical and dramatic forms of verse the only true or noble forms? is Browning, is Juvenal no poet?

But, after all, Mr. Symons is the best critic we have had of Romantic, and even of Realistic, verse. He has lost the irritating precocity and paterism of style which marred his former work; and his criticisms are usually neat, witty, profound, and sensible. He at times is apt to begin to flutter (there is no better word) about the beauty, majesty, golden sweetness, and so forth, of his poets, in the manner of John Addington Symons: but he only does this when led away by enthusiasm for the great names of Blake and Shelley. His verdicts on the minor poets are remarkably sound and convincing; he does not perhaps do justice to George Darley, but his estimates of Leigh Hunt, and the Taylors, his amusing but just condemnations of Southey, Moore, and Scott are admirable. He is the first modern critic to observe the real metrical force of some of Mrs. Hemans' forgotten rhymes, and he makes us clamour for a cheap and good edition of the " Ettrick Shepherd."

In writing of Byron, however, our author, like Mr. Courthope, tends to undue admiration. Byron is a poet who is given to surprising the reader by genuine excellence even in the midst of his absurdest romantic tales: and it has become the fashion to pronounce " Don Juan " to be an excellent, and his most excellent, work. We suspect these fashionables of not having read "Don Juan" through. It is, indeed, a brilliant and amusing work, cunningly versified, yet rather too full of contemporary and unimportant allusions, rather too long and prolix, to hold the attention of the reader. But when we compare it with other works with which in form or tone it challenges comparison we may well ask what it contains which rivals Ariosto and the voyage of Astolfo to the moon ; and we may remark how both its wit, sense and imagination fail when tested by such a poem as Browning's " Blougram"? Byron, as Mr. Saintsbury has truly said, is second-rate for all his merits, and as far below Hogg as a Romantic Poet as he was above him in worldly state and influence. But it is hard to escape from the fascination of his character ; and as a satirist he will surely live.

But, after all, Mr. Symons has made a valiant attempt to judge every poet by the merit of his poetry, and by that alone. He does not write more of their biographies than is inevitable or illuminating: his supreme concern is with their works. With diligent scholarship and an observant, unprejudiced mind he has read through almost every scrap of rhyme written in the forty years of which his book treats. I suppose that in the literature schools of one of our great, or less great, universities, he would obtain, if a candidate, quite a respectable second class.

Let us, however, in fairness consider what, if anything, can be urged in favour of other styles of criticism, in favour of treating poets as politicians, like Courthope, or as characters, like Matthew Arnold. We may say first that to an average mind, Mr. Courthope's book, and books of its class, are liable to be far more interesting than books like that of Mr. Symons, which have a purely aesthetic aim. Had Mr. Courthope called his book a "History of Political Influence in English Poetry," had he been content to trace that influence without making unsuitable remarks on the aesthetic value of poetical productions, his book would be one that could well be praised for its research, its clearness, and its interest. Instead, he has supported that ancient and false critic, popular opinion, which is never a real national verdict—and, if it was, would not be of supreme importance—and is usually nothing but a confused and journalistic distortion of the opinion of a few eminent men of the day. Still worse, under that valiant guise—so popular in these days, so surely a sign of decadence—of being a man who, though a scholar, loves virility, blatant patriotism, and common-sense, he has wronged and insulted the memories of the great. The care, discernment, and mental balance of Arthur Symons is in pleasing contrast to this pompous attitudinizing, and is far more worthy of the high traditions of English literature and of Englishmen.

Yet we often agree with Mr. Courthope when he is not employed in criticism, and especially when he deplores the absence of political interest in modern poetry. He is rather apt to blame the poets: he should blame history. The dearth of proud and eagle-winged forces in this modern age is a calamity for art. Whether these century-old poets preached an idea as Shelley, Byron, and Wordsworth, ran counter to it, as Crabbe, or neglected it, as Keats, they had the inestimable advantage of living in a society rent by the enthusiasm and hatreds of the French Revolution. In those good days Shelley was not an ineffectual angel whose pretty lyrics might be read by simpering girls, but a most effectual Devil, like a socialist of to-day, attacking the very foundations of society. Only during the last year has there arisen in England a political crisis worthy of the pen: and in this revived bitterness of strife lies at least some hope for the future of English poetry.

THE GOLDEN JOURNEY TO SAMARKAND[1]

PREFACE

FEELING some explanation of my attitude towards the art of poetry might assist critics and interest friends, I hoped to be able to expound in this preface my theory. But I found I had no new theory. All I can do is to praise a very simple theory of poetry which has for me a unique attraction—that of the French " Parnasse." A careful study of this theory, however old-fashioned it may by now have become in France, would, I am convinced, benefit English critics and poets, for both our poetic criticism and our poetry are in chaos. It is a Latin theory, and therefore the more likely to supply the defects of the Saxon genius. It would do English poetry—which is to-day as far beneath the French as it was of old above it—and English literary criticism, which has never been comparable with that of our neighbours, no harm to take, as Dan Chaucer took of old, a lesson from the Continent.

Good poetry has obviously been written on other theories than the Parnassian. It has been written

[1] Published by arrangement with Mr. Martin Secker.

with no theory at all. It has been written with very strange theories. Good poetry has been Catholic like Crashaw's, and Protestant like Milton's, and mystic like Blake's, and atheistic like the " De Rerum Natura." Good poetry has been full of high moral sentiments, like Wordsworth's, of highly immoral sentiments, like Byron's, or quite amoral sentiments, like Herrick's. Good poetry has been written in boorish speech, like that of Barnes, or in elegant diction, like that of Pope.

No worthless writer will be redeemed by the excellence of the poetic theory he may chance to hold.

But that a sound theory can produce sound practice, and exercise a beneficent effect on writers of genius, has been repeatedly proved in the short but glorious history of the " Parnasse."

The Parnassian School was a classical reaction against the perfervid sentimentality and extravagance of some French Romantics. The Romantics in France, as in England, had done their powerful work, and infinitely widened the scope and enriched the language of poetry. It remained for the Parnassians to raise the technique of their art to a height which should enable them to express the subtlest ideas in powerful and simple verse. But the real meaning of the term Parnassian may be best understood from considering what is definitely not Parnassian. To be didactic, like Wordsworth, to write dull poems of unwieldy length, to bury, like Tennyson or Browning, poetry of exquisite beauty in monstrous realms of vulgar, feeble, or obscure versifying, to overlay fine work with gross and irrelevant egoism, like Victor Hugo, would be abhorrent, and rightly so, to members of this school. On the other hand, the finest work of many great English poets, especially Milton, Keats, Matthew Arnold, and Tennyson, is written in the same tradition as the work of the great French school: and one can but wish that the two latter poets had had something of a definite theory to guide them in self-criticism. Tennyson would never have published "Locksley Hall," and Arnold might have refrained from spoiling his finest sonnets by astonishing cacophonies.

There are, of course, many splendid forms of passionate or individual poetry which are not Parnassian. The work of Shelley and Browning, of Rossetti, or Villon or Verlaine, however perfect, is too emotional, individual or eccentric, to have any affinity with the Parnassian School.

The French Parnassian has a tendency to use traditional forms, and even to employ classical subjects. His desire in writing poetry is to create beauty: his inclination is toward a beauty somewhat statuesque. He is apt to be dramatic and objective rather than intimate. The enemies of the Parnassians have accused them of cultivating unemotional frigidity and upholding an austere view of perfection. The unanswerable answers to all criticism are the works of Hérédia, Leconte de Lisle, Samain, Henri de Régnier, and Jean Moréas. Compare the early works of the latter poet, written under the influence of the Symbolists, with his " Stances," if you would see what excellence of theory can do when it has genius to work on. Read the works of Hérédia if you would understand how conscious and perfect artistry, far from stifling inspiration, fashions it into shapes of unimaginable beauty. Hérédia wrote one volume of sonnets. They are traditional in form. Their subjects are classical or historical. They are utterly remote from modern life and turmoil. Each one evokes a distinct, complete, and delicate image of the past. And yet there is hardly one of them that is not immortal poetry, and the passion that breathes in the sonnets on Cleopatra is of such fiery intensity that I doubt if in all lyric poetry it would be excelled.

To have preached a Parnassian doctrine in the age of Pope would have been superfluous: to have attempted to restrain therewith the impetuous torrent of Elizabethan or Victorian production would have been impossible. But at the present moment there can be no doubt that English poetry stands in need of some such saving doctrine to redeem it from the formlessness and the didactic tendencies which are now in fashion. As for English criticism, can it not learn from the Parnassian or any tolerable theory of poetic art to examine the beauty and not the " message " of poetry?

This importunity of the " message," this " old Puritan spirit," has corrupted nearly all our artists, from William Wordsworth down to the latest writers of manly tales in verse. If we have preaching to do, in heaven's name let us call it a sermon and write it in prose. It is not the poet's business to save man's soul, but to make it worth saving. It is not his business to make wise reflections about the social and moral problems of the day, but, whether inspired by a slum window in Camden Town or by an old volume picked up for a soldo in the streets of Florence, to make beautiful the tragedy, and tragic the beauty, of man's life. Many of our great English poets have preached moral theories, or expounded in verse their philosophies of life; but it is to be remembered that what endures of their work is that portion where, despite themselves, they wrote like poets. However few great poets have written with a clear theory of art for art's sake, it is by that theory alone that their work has been, or can be, judged ; and rightly so if we remember that art embraces all life and all humanity, and sees, in the temporary and fleeting doctrines of conservative or revolutionary, only the human grandeur or passion that inspires them.

To this volume, written with the single intention of creating beauty, now the Moslem East, now Greece and her islands has furnished a setting. Those who are for ever seeking for what they call profundity of inspiration are welcome to burrow in my verse and extract something, if they will, as barren as the few cheap copy-book headings to which they once reduced the genius of Browning; in the attitude to life expressed in these pages, in the Poet's appreciation of this transient world, the flowers and men and mountains that decorate it so superbly, they will probably find but little edification.

BEYROUT,
April, 1913.

THE PUBLIC AS ART CRITIC

IT is the fashion among certain amiable writers of the present day to exalt public opinion and approve public taste. True merit, they cry, is crowned at last by the civic laurel: public opinion works slowly but surely, and popular applause is the supreme test of value. Of these amiable writers Mr. Chesterton is by far the most conspicuous and cunning. The form and style, that is to say, the beauties of literature, are nothing to him. He blasphemes the very name of art. He gushes about Watts as if he were the peer of Leonardo da Vinci. As if he had never read "Endymion" or "Isabella," he remarks that Keats was one of those people who are incapable of writing bad poetry. Keats, the most desperately careless and slovenly of all great poets; Keats, who wrote "Why in the name of glory were they proud!" But Mr. Chesterton is a democrat, and this is the democratic view of poetry. Shakespeare was in some respects a typical honest middle-class Englishman. What a joyous discovery for Mr. Chesterton! Quick follows the inevitable generalization. "The first-class artist considers himself the equal of other men, like Shakespeare." And Michael Angelo? And Beethoven? And Goethe? Are they all third-class then? "The third-class artist thinks himself superior to other men, like Whistler." The whole doctrine of Mr. Chesterton is a fraud: his whole argument for democracy in art amounts to this: "Dickens was a good writer and popular: therefore, good writers are popular."

Let us examine the real facts of the case. We must establish first of all that there is an actual standard in art. If you think William Watson a better poet than William Shakespeare, your opinion is not merely curious, it is wrong. Should you maintain your opinion was correct, and you had every right to hold it, I might attempt to prove your error to you by appealing to the laws of art. But I admit the proof would be abominably hard and difficult, not because art has no laws, but because it has such terribly diffi- cult and complex ones, like all great human institu- tions. But that a standard exists, and that criticism is not a mere question of personal taste, can be shown by one conclusive proof. It is this: The more a man studies an art the more he is compelled to agree with those who have made the same study before him, and to admit that the famous names are the great ones. He may perhaps differ from the general view in valuing Matthew Arnold a little less, and Pope a little more: but the striking thing about critics is not that they diverge, but that despite all new brilliant, and impartial treatments of their subject, they agree.

Well then, you say, if the most famous names are really the greatest, public opinion, which gives men fame, is the infallible critic after all. But it is not public opinion which bestows fame. The admiration for great names is imposed on the public by a small band of earnest critics who have a passion for art, who understand its technique, who study its history. It is they who fight the long battle against the Philistines; and having a righteous cause at heart, they usually win. For the public is not so foolishly self-complacent as Mr. Chesterton imagines. The public knows it has its own great business to do, and has not the leisure or knowledge to discover artistic secrets: and it wisely follows the lead of the expert whenever it can find one.

For an expert is needed. Criticism is almost as difficult as creation, and there is no royal road to the comprehension of the beautiful. No one can understand music, who knows nothing of the rules of harmony; no one can fully appreciate a picture, who has not some idea how lumps of paint are stuck on canvas. A play or a novel, I admit, has a much wider, more direct and human appeal, and a good unspecialized average intelligence is more likely to succeed in its estimate of literature than in its estimate of painting or music. But even literary criticism is largely a technical affair, and the criticism of poetry is the hardest branch of the science that exists. This critic must have an ear no less subtle than the poet's to mark the apt spacing of the consonants and the noble procession of the vowels. Words must call up to him all their sweet associations of sound and sense. The word "road" must mean for him not merely one particular road, but all the roads in the world whereon men walk like pilgrims from the grey of dawn to the terror of the sunset. "House" must suggest to him all the habitations of clay, brick, stone, or snow, where men have lived, wept, died, or played with their children round the fire. The word "tree" for him as for the poet must signify a thing that was once worshipped, where still maybe hides a nut-brown Dryad, and whose falling leaves symbolize the end of all our dreaming.

The critic of poetry must know all the minutiae of the technique not so much that he may be able to carp at faults as that he may realize perfection. He must know his art so well that he feels at once and instinctively, not after reflection merely, whether the lines he is reading ring true. Yet he must not be a pedant: he must have deep experience of life, he must be a man of character. In the true sense of the word he must be moral. He must prepare for his task austerely: it is a high one. He must cast aside for an hour his own puritanism and prejudice, his petty, even his noble beliefs about the world, and become receptive of the impressions of others to the extreme limit of human nature. He must not condemn poems because they are morbid, profane, or deal with what the Manchester Watch Committee (who forbade Maud Allan to dance in their beautiful and virtuous town) would call unpleasant subjects. He will know that art is divided, not into decadent and healthy, classic and romantic, but into the two mighty divisions of Good and Bad, and that these divisions alone hold true. One great dogma alone he must hold—that human life is passionately interesting in all its phases, that over the filthiest by-ways the sky of night must stretch its flowery mantle of stars. The critic must be of purer mould than the poet himself. He must have a profound love for man, not the vague enthusiasm of the humanitarian but a vivid delight in all the men in the world, men sinful, men splendid, men coarse, or cowardly, or pathetic. And in all the phenomena of nature, sordid or shining, the background to our tragedy, he must admire, if not the beauty, then the force, the law, the cruelty, and the power. And with this enthusiasm in his soul he will bitterly condemn dullness, weakness, bad workmanship, vulgar thought, shoddy sentiment as being slanders on mankind; and in this sense and this sense only—that it is the glory of man—great art is moral.

Yet though so few can be good critics of art, I do not mean that art is only for the elect. It is indisputable that thousands honestly and genuinely enjoy, admire, and love certain works of art which they know to be considered great. How should it be otherwise? A spark of the divine is in us all; some sentiment for the sea, the wind and sunshine, for death and for the ancient story of love. Every life is a poem acted: of our trivial affairs painters construct their canvases, and poets weave their songs. We are whacked as children—Gozzoli has painted us; our sister has a music lesson—Terborch has drawn her with the light shining on her earnest face: our mother peels potatoes: Chardin has painted her, and the potatoes, so that we feel we never knew what a potato was like before. We fall in love and feel that lyrical exaltation we cannot express, but we know our love is that of Paolo for Francesca, though she lives at No. 7 Brixton Gardens. We enact our own tragedy and die, grand as Lear himself, bound on the same path as the heroic kings of old.

But granted that the people have the emotions from which great artists draw the substance of their work, have a vague passionate yearning towards those images of beauty which art has fixed, yet the people never know how fine a fine work is, because they cannot see the vileness of a base one. I once heard a shop-girl say that the two plays she liked best were " The Silver King," and " that one where the black man gets jealous and kills his girl." She meant " Othello." Well, the sun of art may shine so strong that the blindest eyes are dazzled, but only the eagles comprehend the glory of that disc. The novelist of the people is Marie Corelli, their poet Ella Wheeler Wilcox, their artist Blair Leighton, their musician Paul Rubens. Mr. Chesterton will doubtless say it is because the people are so nice that they admire these marvels: that they honestly think Miss Corelli profound, Miss Wilcox passionate, Mr. B. Leighton chivalrous, and Mr. Rubens lyrical and sparkling. The people are pleasant and fascinating, I readily agree, though I dislike those who parade their affection for the populace, and their love of Christmasses, children, and the homely virtues in order to make the said populace think what ripping fellows they are. But you cannot appreciate both Blair Leighton and Euphronios. If you cannot see that the " Epic of Hades " (it sells by the hundred thousand) is beneath contempt, you are not fit to read " Paradise Lost." If you don't know how bad the bad is you can never tell how good the good is.

But if the middle classes should exclaim " Our gods are better than these," I should reply that the devotees of Robert Hichens and the thumpers of Rachmaninoff preludes are in a far worse case than the jolly mass of the people who simply want to be amused. Many of the middle class falsely imagine they have taste : they do terrible dis-service to art by buying pretentious and vulgar stuff and setting up a hideous clamour if their sense of propriety is outraged. Say there were ten good pictures in the Neo-Impressionist exhibition, were there six in last year's academy? Yet no one said that that exhibition was an insult to the public, or that those coarse portraits of King Edward were a slur on the dignity of Empire. Or admit that Salome is a faulty opera; do you shriek and squeal when some tinkling atrocity like the " Cavalleria Rusticana " holds the stage? Where rose your cultured voices when the new Victoria and Albert Museum emerged in unassuming ugliness, with those silly little statues stuck round in a row, indistinguishable save by their beards. Is not that building an insult to the taste of the British Public? An insult we shall have to endure some hundred years or longer.

In the old days when the aristocracy really cared

for art, and pork-butchers cared only for their pork, there was less chatter and more appreciation for true greatness. Art lives on to-day, but in noble retirement, too proud to ask for pence. The artist hears all around him infinite rubbish talked about his art, and imagines for the moment that the middle classes are sincere, and will be willing at least to hear his symphony or read his book. You soon undeceive him, you middle classes. You, who have let, are letting, and will let your poets die of hunger, continue to buy your pretty editions of the classics and to frame photogravures of the "Sistine Madonna" over your mantelshelves. You know quite well that vital art bores you and you have never understood it.

PAUL FORT, THE "PRINCE OF POETS"[1]

PHILOMEL[2]

From the French of Paul Fort

O SING, in heart of silence hiding near,
Thou whom the roses bend their heads to hear!
In silence down the moonlight slides her wing:
Will no rose breathe while Philomel doth sing?
No breath—and deeper yet the perfume grows:
The voice of Philomel can slay a rose:
The song of Philomel on nights serene
Implores the gods who roam in shades unseen,
But never calls the roses, whose perfume
Deepens and deepens, as they wait their doom.
Is it not silence whose great bosom heaves?
Listen, a rose-tree drops her quiet leaves.

Now silence flashes lightning like a storm:
Now silence is a cloud, and cradled warm
By risings and by fallings of the tune
That Philomel doth sing, as shines the moon,

---

[1] The new anthology of Paul Fort's poems "Choix de Ballades françaises" (Figuière, 6 fr.), may be recommended to intending readers whom our poet's prolific output might otherwise bewilder and repel. In it Paul Fort has for the first time properly classified his work.

[2] "Philomel" is included in this volume by arrangement with Mr. Martin Secker.

—A bird's or some immortal voice from Hell
There is no breath to die with, Philomel!—
And yet the world has changed without a breath.
The moon lies heavy on the roses' death,
And every rosebush droops its leafy crown.
A gust of roses has gone sweeping down.
The panicked garden drives her leaves about :
The moon is masked : it flares and flickers out.
O shivering petals on your lawn of fear,
Turn down to Earth and hear what you shall hear.
A beat, a beat, a beat beneath the ground,
And hurrying beats, and one great beat profound.
A heart is coming close : I have heard pass
The noise of a great Heart upon the grass.
The petals reel. Earth opens: from beneath
The ashen roses on their lawn of death,
Raising her peaceful brow, the grand and pale
Demeter listens to the nightingale.

WHAT a large contribution French literature
of the last ten years has made to the splendid unity achieved by France in face of the
great but long foreseen danger of war, how firmly that
reaction to heroic ideals of discipline and religion has
been led by men like Barrès and Maurras, is hardly
realized in England at all, where the Press, choked
with articles on unimportant and obscure curiosities
like Strindberg[1] or Tagore, has no time to attend to
the one foreign literature worth reading. Indeed,
the only modern French writer known in England is
Anatole France, imagined a solitary star in a waste of
night !

[1] Mr. E. Gosse, who wrote a charming criticism of Paul Fort
some years ago, has lately given a crushing opinion on Strindberg in the first number of the "New Weekly." [Flecker's note.]

It cannot be pretended that Paul Fort has been a direct leader of this renovating movement in France; indeed, it would be vain to expect the Poet to take the didactic lead. A poet should teach discipline by the severity of his verse, courage by the strength of his line, honour by the scrupulous sincerity of his achievement. But that is merely to say a poet should be a good poet. Paul Fort gives us more than this— he gives us the new spirit of France, that brave common-sense that bursts out in gaiety and imagination, and gives the impression that though the world is deadly serious it is still disreputably young.

The possibility of the creation of poetry like this may be said to mark a revolution in the French mentality. A few years ago French critics did really and honestly consider that literature and civilization had reached their last stage of cynical corruption. But of late the whole youth of France seem to have been recaptured by the old ideals of the peasant, the soldier, the priest; and though neither militarist nor clerical, Paul Fort yet has all the irrepressible hopefulness of the young generation that drives on the soldiers of France in charge after charge against their monstrous enemy. For him a few mechanical inventions or scientific improvements have not spoilt the sunrise; and accepting the civilization of to-day as Homer accepted that of three thousand years ago, he celebrates simply, but with startling novelty of inspiration, the scenery and actors of that once so pleasant stage—the France he lives in.

The Prince of Poets is no Futurist, though Marinetti

has bidden his followers admire him. He writes no odes on aeroplanes or automobiles. He does not lay a particular stress on the mechanical side of modern life, being too fond of his contemporaries to insult them by considering them less interesting than machines. The minor poets of the Futurist School, in their struggle to escape those trammels of the centuries which oppress all timorous minds, adopt any childish eccentricity of metre, language, or subject that comes into their heads. At the same time they impose upon themselves a harder law than any Academy ever yet invented for the suppression of that free play which is so necessary for the expansion of genius. They are not allowed by their leaders to write a line, except in derision, about the past. Paul Fort has described the past as well as the present; but when, as often, he deals with modern life, he has courage enough to envisage it in its proper relation to the past, and genius enough to reveal its fascination without distorting its reality. He is only able to do this because he has dug down to the bed-rock of human nature, because he understands the good old basic things of life—the soil, the sun, the rain; the labour, sorrows, and songs of the people. He can himself actually write Folk Songs—a unique achievement for a great literary artist—folk songs that seem as if they must be traditional, must have been composed hundreds of years ago. When one thinks of the evolution of French poetry during the last few generations, with its imposing array of schools—Romantics, Parnassians, Symbolists, Unanimists, and the rest—one realizes what superb detachment is required (not to mention other and higher qualities) for a Frenchman and a Parisian to write a poem as finely unadorned as this:

Si toutes les filles du monde voulaient s' donner la main tout
    autour de la mer elles pourraient faire une ronde.
Si tous les gars du monde voulaient bien être marins, ils f'raient
    avec leurs barques un joli pont sur l'onde.
Alors on pourrait faire une ronde autour du monde si tous les
    gens du monde voulaient s' donner la main.

It is natural that a poet so much haunted by the peasant should have sought inspiration from mediaeval France. Paul Fort's longest work, "le Roman de Louis XI," is a fantasy half in verse, half in prose, remarkably close in feeling and in style to Rabelais. The hero is presented with humour and sympathy, for the King, who had nothing but a shrewd wit to save his impoverished kingdom from the menace of the bellicose, parading, pompous Duke of Burgundy, is a man after the author's heart. French critics have quoted as a masterpiece of pathos the little scene in which Louis discovers that his son Joachim is dead. But the most memorable passage in the book is the hilarious description of the siege of Beauvais, with its catalogue of the missiles (beginning with paving stones and ending with complete houses), which the besieged dropped with gorgeously noisy effects on to the heads of the besiegers. It must have been this passage that awoke in Marinetti an admiration for Paul Fort, for granted that realizing in poetry the effect of a tremendous noise be a Futurist ideal, Paul Fort has certainly beaten Marinetti on his own ground.

The latter's "Battle of Tripoli" is very thin piping compared with the "Siege of Beauvais."

Yet neither the excellent "Louis XI" nor that ambitious poem sequence, "l'Aventure Eternelle," is the real achievement of Paul Fort. It is by his lyrics that he will be remembered, lyrics so numerous, so brilliant, and so diverse, that even briefly to discuss their leading characteristics is rather a bewildering task. However, of these characteristics, the most obvious and pervading one beyond any doubt is humour—humour of the great lyrical quality, which can remind us at times of Heine, of Cervantes, of Browning, and, as will be hereafter observed, most specially of Shakespeare—yet a humour which combines with an impudence almost English a lightness entirely French:

LES BALEINES

Du temps qu'on allait encore aux baleines, si loin qu'ça faisait mat'lot, pleurer nos belles, y avait sur chaque route un Jésus en croix, y avait des marquis converts de dentelles, y avait la Sainte-Vierge et y avait le Roi !

Du temps qu'on allait encore aux baleines, si loin qu'ça faisait mat'lot, pleurer nos belles, y avait des marins qui avaient la foi, et des grands seigneurs qui crachaient sur elle, y avait la Sainte-Vierge et y avait le Roi !

Eh bien, à présent tout le monde est content, c'est pas pour dire, mat'lot, mais on est content ! . . . y a plus de grands seigneurs ni d'Jésus qui tiennent, y a la république et y a le président, et y a plus de baleines !

A still more extravagant poem, called "The One-Eyed Cat," recalls nothing written in the French

language except the " Poèmes en prose " of Baudelaire :

> La femme est aux varechs, l'homme est à la Guyane. Et la
> petite maison est seule tout le jour.
>
> Seule ? Mais à travers les persiennes vertes, on voit luire
> dans l'ombre comme une goutte de mer.
>
> Quand le bagne est à l'homme, la mer est à la femme, et la
> petite maison au chat borgne tout le jour.

Among scores of poems in this vein the reader may
be specially referred to " Le Marchand de Sable,"
" La Reine à la mer," " Le Paysan et son âne," perhaps the most amusing of all, and to one unaccount-
ably excluded from the anthology, " Le petit roi du
Nord." Similar in humorous treatment, but more
subtle, are some of the poems on Shakespearean
characters, to which Englishmen will turn with special
interest. " Hamlet " begins thus :

> Hamlet, que la folie des autres importune, a fait le tour du
> monde mais dans le clair de lune il retrouve Elseneur qu'il
> n'avait pas quitté.
> Hamlet a fait le tour du monde, comme il fait tout, en pensée.

Still more exquisitely subtle is Seigneur Fortinbras :

> Moi que l'on attendait, j'entre en disant ma phrase. . . . Je
> viens clore le drame avec un clairon d'or—tout seul—car mon
> immense armée ne viendra pas, que voulez-vous ? Je l'ai perdue
> dans les décors ombreux de la coulisse. Enfin ! Taratata !

The genius of all this is near enough to the pathetic,
and Paul Fort is as clever as Verlaine or de Banville
in catching what may be called the Pierrot mood.

S

"The Dead Clown" is rather an obvious subject,
charmingly treated; the "Song of the little Valet who
hanged himself" is as delicately mysterious as a lyric
by Mr. Yeats. His masterpiece of humorous pathos
is the "Complaint of the Little White Horse," who
worked so bravely on in a country of black rain where
there was never any spring:

Il est mort sans voir le beau temps: qu'il avait donc du courage!

Paul Fort has more ambitious flights than these,
but his humour seldom deserts him; indeed, it often
breaks out in unexpected places with a most startling
effect. His "Poèmes Marins" and ballads of modern
Paris have plenty of laughter in their realism. The
"Poèmes Marins" need special attention, as being,
perhaps, the most powerful volume the poet has produced. They are ballad poems of modern life, somewhat in the tradition handed down from Béranger to
Richepin and the singers of Montmartre. But Paul
Fort's sailors—sentimental, coarse, amusing, passionate—put Richepin's tedious "Gueux" out of court.
They hate every one who is not washed clean by the
sea—farmers, beggars, priests, soldiers, opoponaxed
Parisians. And, above all, says one of them, "tu me
dégoûtes, ma garce." It is not gallant, but French
mariners are a privileged race and know it. "Je ne
suis pas marine, mais il n'y a que les marins," cries a
mountain lass in her sailor's arms. Excellent, too, is
the young fisherman who complains to his mother
that he loves three girls at once, and they *will* not
understand! But there are savage and bitter poems

in the book, and the description of the drunkard who
kills his wife is terrible enough for a Russian novel:

> Ne gueule pas comme ça, l'ciel n'est pas solide. Y tourne
> comme un fou: le bon Dieu s'est soûlé. Qui c'est ça, tais-toi
> . . . bois ton rhum salé. Eh bien quoi? . . . t'es morte? Tiens,
> tu n'as plus de rides!
> Ma petite chérie, ma petite chérie! T'es morte, moi je suis
> soûl. L'bon Dieu bat la crème. Toutes les étoiles tournent.
> Y a des loups dans l'eau qu'ont d'l'or plein leur gueule. T'auras
> pas ma paye!

A striking contrast to this realistic work is afforded
by the poems which he has in this anthology called
" Hymnes"—heroic odes in praise of nature. They
are powerful in expression and grand in conception,
but one of them, a poem called " Le Dauphin," is so
passionately inspired, as to make the magnificence
and brilliance of the other " Hymnes" seem almost
frozen in comparison. Swinburne himself has no better
song on the joy of swimming and the enchantment of
the sea. The chase of the dolphins as the swimmer
" turns with the wheel of the sun" among the waves,
the seaweed, and the flying fish, is not so much described, as seen and heard in the sparkling, splashing
verses, while in the vision of the sea's floor the poem
assumes a note of grandeur—one of the rarest notes
of Paul Fort's brilliant lyre:

> Je vois! (la petite mort est entrée dans mon cœur) j'ai revu
> tous ces monts soulevés de douleurs. En eux la mer contente
> sa destinée sauvage. Elle fouille la terre, elle s'accouple aux
> laves, ensemence leur sein de toute sa vigueur, et mille bouches
> de feu bavent des coquillages. Volcans, brûlez la mer des feux
> de votre cœur! Les étincelles vivent: ô que de poissons nagent!

Les étincelles meurent et c'est là votre ouvrage : vous attirez les morts qui vont en vous reprendre la chaleur et la Vie. O cendres, cendres, cendres ! Etincelles ! … et déjà, vos rochers sont couverts de coraux, de varechs, d'épais ombrages verts, de crabes fourmillants et de ces belles pieuvres envahissant la mer de leurs bras amoureux ; les hippocampes noirs s'échappent de vos feux ; la bleue holothurie scintille : c'est votre œuvre ; le bas limon s'étoile à l'exemple des cieux. Qu'un jour tout cela meure, vous attendez les cendres. La mer, buvant la mort, devient phosphorescente. Vous l'aspirez. Vos feux déjà, se renouvellent—et les oiseaux marins volent jusqu'au soleil !

The "Hymnes" lead us naturally to the poems dealing with classical subjects, grouped in the new anthology as "Hymnes héroïques," "Eglogues," and "Chants paniques." These lyrics are hardly the most characteristic work of the author, whose sympathies are mediaeval rather than Greek. Paul Fort sings of Jason, of Hercules, of Orpheus simply because he loves all delightful tales, not because he has a special appreciation of the classical world. But he is at his best when he deals with Morpheus, with the nymphs and fauns—with all those suggestive whispering little gods who have haunted Christian Europe far more tenaciously than the white Olympians. One of these pictures is unforgettable—the old faun clumsily dancing round the frozen lake, trying to reawaken the old magic voices which have abandoned the forest for ever.

Yet, though we hold these "classical" poems to be a mere side issue of Paul Fort's genius, what great poems they really are—"le Voyage de Jason," "Orphée," "les Néréides," with what freshness does the poet attack the age-worn themes, with what humour does he charm Olympus! It is surely with these poems, moreover, that we should class the most beautiful lyric Paul Fort has ever written, the haunting " Philomèle." [1]

English readers who study for themselves the " Poèmes Marins " will be bound to remark the extraordinary, almost pagan innocence of their author, which seems to enable him to deal with any subject under the sun without prudery and without licentiousness. Certainly Paul Fort never feels himself obliged, like so many modern English writers, to adopt a tone of fictitious manliness to palliate anything which a very timorous curate might find shocking. And he is no less innocent when he deals with the externals of religion. " Coxcomb," half poem, half story, is a masterpiece of merry humour—blasphemous only as Benozzo Gozzoli blasphemes when he turns the laughing girls and boys of Florence into saints, angels, and virgins. To the truly and deeply religious mind, far more dangerous than this quaint irreverence is the utilizing of the aesthetic beauty of Christianity to decorate poems that are not quite sincere, a moral fault from which our author is not entirely free, and in which our own Pre-Raphaelites revelled.[2]

[1] A verse translation of " Philomèle " precedes this article.

[2] Yet what rings false in these thrilling lines from " Le Plus doux Chant " ?

" Mais oh ! le chant que j'aime. . . . Il me faut l'air câlin plus nonchalant et triste dont Marie enchanta l'ouie au petit Christ, et que siffla si doux Joseph le menuisier qu'il fit naître à ce chant ' le Rêve de l'Enfant."

" Oh les plus frêles sons ! le suprême chant que répétait Jésus au ciel de Bethléem, et que les Syriennes, éveillant les cithares, murmuraient—s'y penchant—aux ciels de leurs fontaines ! "

To discover the real religion or philosophy of Paul Fort, we must turn to one of his later poems, "Vivre en Dieu," a work more interesting in thought than happy as poetry, in which he has made a direct, but still amusing, attempt to state and arrange his views on God and the world. The divine function, according to the poet, is to dream, for dream or imagination is a creative force. There is no creative dream in stone, but everything that is alive has a certain power of vision and is, therefore, God: " l'herbe est un Dieu hâtif doué de rêve ayant une âme visionnaire." Trees are gods, men are gods—but there are degrees. The Poet, who above other men possesses the faculty of creative imagination, is the greatest god on earth. All lives dream each other into existence; "no other explanation of the universe," adds the writer with his accustomed laugh. " Messieurs, levez votre chapeau."

This conception of the universe is more arresting at least than the admired Wordsworthian pantheism; but it is neither particularly new nor important, taken purely as philosophy. It possesses, nevertheless, both personal interest and poetical force, being very well adapted to provide a logical background to the inexhaustible gaiety and lovableness of the poet's disposition. There is always something religious in Paul Fort's attitude to Nature; his whole work is bathed in spiritual sunshine, and when he is closest to tragedy, the consolation he evokes wears the traditional Christian raiment:

Do not believe in death. Here are the birds who have flown out of their cages, which were the dark and silent woods. Shed no more vain tears. Heaven is singing like your soul, is dumb no longer—and here is radiant Death.

And here is luminous and tuneful Death, and here is Life. Here is the pearl of your soul that an angel of that calm world is threading, and here the radiant music of the Archangel's song.

. . . .

A vast section of Paul Fort's work is devoted to delightful poems in which the country towns and villages near Paris are described with incomparable charm and sentiment. The poet wanders from Reclose, from Velizy, from Morcerf (whose sweet name reminds him of fairies dancing round a sleeping Knight), to Nemours:

Pure Nemours, silver seal on France's noblest page, or great lily of the isle, is not thy destiny, white town, soul of a sky like pearl, to school in elegance the proud world itself?

to la Ferté Milon, where seven distinct houses claim to be the birthplace of Racine, like the seven islands which disputed Homer, and to a hundred little towns beside—and we have their history, their legends, the girl at the window, the ducks in the pond, the ghosts in the castle, the auction in the town hall, all set forth in a whirl of humour or sentiment. But there is pathos now in the exquisite poems on Senlis, which recently, as a result of special and atrocious barbarity on the part of the Germans, has been irretrievably destroyed, Notre Dame and all.

SENLIS MATINALE

JE sors. La ville a-t-elle disparu ce matin ? Où s'est-elle envolée ? Par quel vent dans quelle île ? Je la retrouve, mais n'ose plus étendre les mains. Senlis est vaporeuse comme une mousseline.

Moi, déchirer Senlis ? Prenons garde. Où est-elle ? Toits et murs sont un transparent réseau de brume. Notre-Dame livre à l'air sa gorge de dentelle, son cou si fin, son sein léger couleur de lune.

Où bat l'heure irréelle, que seuls comptent les anges, tant l'écho s'en étouffe dans l'oreiller du ciel fait des plumes doucement étendues de leurs ailes, où Dieu repose un front qui vers Senlis se penche.

Alas, Senlis is torn, and the tower of Notre Dame will shine in the morning mist no longer!

It is for the glory of France that these poems were written—and such passionate patriotism is almost too personal a thing to be discussed by the foreign critic. One would naturally conclude that Paul Fort, considering the great patriotic reaction, would be at least as popular in France. were it on the score of this section of his work alone, as, say, Mr. Masefield in England. One could well imagine such a national, direct, simple, and humorous poet holding a position in his lifetime somewhat similar to that which Carducci used to hold in Italy. Yet Paul Fort—and this would appear to be a very curious fact of literary history—however much he may be the idol of the young literary circles who this year elected him Prince of Poets, however numerous and enthusiastic may be the articles on his work which appear from time to time in the literary reviews, is hardly more known to the general public than was the classicist Moréas or, to take an English example, that fine poet Mr. De la Mare.

Moreover, the reason for this comparative neglect,

for these second and third editions of work which one
would expect to sell by the ten thousand, cannot
possibly be that Paul Fort stands in any way apart
from his time. Nationalism, regionalism, mediaevalism,
the love of country and the soil have been the very
breath of the gospel of Maurice Barrès, and of a thousand lesser pens, and are enormously in fashion. Again,
while Paul Fort is perhaps hardly like Barrès, a Catholic,
yet he has an unshaken belief in the Catholic virtues
and a sure insight into Catholic ideals. The antipathy
—almost hatred—of the Parisian mind for humour
may have something to do with the neglect of Paul
Fort. Humour to many Frenchmen is a gross extravagance, and they are all a little apt to take poetry
too seriously. Yet there is plenty of good work in
Paul Fort which is not humorous, and one is driven
to the only conclusion possible, queer as it may sound
to English readers, that the chief reason of this comparative neglect is to be found in our poet's metrical
peculiarities. As will have been seen by the extracts
given in French, Paul Fort has abandoned the general
practice of writing out poetry line by line and writes
it out verse by verse instead. He also has a habit of
letting his poetry " degenerate " either into a prose
with internal rhymes, similar to that Oriental prose of
which the curious can find a horrible parody in Beacons-
field's " Alroy," or (as often in the longer poems) into
pure prose. In addition to this our poet frequently
disregards the rule that the final *e* mute counts as a
syllable for poetic purposes. This is a licence frequently
used in popular poetry and songs, but Paul Fort does

not take the trouble to mark the suppression of the
sham syllable in the regular way by omitting the
e mute and substituting an apostrophe. Indeed the
effect if he did so would be very ugly and tiring.
These innovations do not seem to an English student
very terrible, and indeed about half of Paul Fort's
poetry could perfectly well be printed out in lines and
be read as popular poetry, and no one would any
more dream of cavilling at it as a breach of tradition
than at Richepin's:

> Il y avait un' fois un pauvre gas
> Qui aimait cell' qui n' l' aimait pas.

Besides, it might be observed, there is nothing very
revolutionary in the printing of verse as prose. It
might even be called, on the contrary, a return to the
old tradition, for a monkish scribe copying Virgil
would go to greater lengths than our author in
jumbling up the lines—would, in fact, jumble up the
very words.

This is not to say, however, that Paul Fort's
practice in this respect is perfectly reasonable and
wise. The greatest enthusiast for his work must
admit that in the longer poems it is often very
puzzling to know, without careful scrutiny, whether
the poet has any rhythmical intentions or not. It is
also invariably difficult to discover the words which
are intended to rhyme. It is, at least, doubtful
whether the "half-way house" and quick transition
from verse into prose, at which the author says he
aims by his peculiar typography, would not be better

served by simply printing verse as verse and prose as prose. The only real advantage about the system, as far as one can see, is that the reader is imperceptibly led to read the lines more rapidly, and that the licences taken, which include, besides those already mentioned, the occasional use of very vague assonance in the place of rhyme,[1] look less alarming. Certainly the innovation attracted attention and discussion to the poet's early work, but unfortunately, as years went on, critics continued to discuss the metre instead of the poetry, and the French, with their passion for order and tradition, are still very worried about this comparatively trifling aspect of a great achievement—so that for many Frenchmen even to-day Paul Fort is "the poet who writes in prose," and is unjustly confounded with a thousand maudlin writers of amateurish prose poems. I believe that if he were to publish his shorter lyrics, printed in the old-established way, they would be received with immense enthusiasm, not only by a literary clique but by the whole French nation.

. . . .

The ranking of poets is a tedious and rather childish pastime, which many critics at once deride and enjoy; yet there is somehow an undoubted pleasure in constructing a hierarchy, in picturing modern French poetry to oneself as being led by two great chiefs, Henri de Régnier and Paul Fort—two men of genius strikingly dissimilar to each other, and

[1] Assonance is frequently used by Francis Jammes and even by the classical Henri de Régnier.

only alike in towering above all possible rivals of the present day. Unfortunately, this is no very high compliment, for if we count Verhaeren as a Belgian—and even he seems to write steadily worse year by year—there is very little left in modern French poetry, since the untimely deaths of Samain and Moréas, which calls for more than respect, outside the work of these two men of genius. Exception must be made in favour of the delicate and charming spirit of Francis Jammes.

But a more interesting and more legitimate part of the critic's task is the study of affinity. In criticizing this author one is apt to make endless comparisons with the great writers, and especially with the great humorists, of the past. But, strangely enough, it is Shakespeare himself who, more than any other writer, living or dead, is recalled by the work of Paul Fort. In this assertion, of course, no comparison of value is implied; the Tragic and the Sublime are not regions into which Paul Fort has entered. It is to the Shakespeare of the " Midsummer Night's Dream," not to the Shakespeare of " Macbeth," that our Frenchman has affinity. But the affinity is very striking, nevertheless; there is something deep in the nature of both poets that positively coincides. Is it, perhaps, their exuberance that makes them kin, their bravado air of looking at the world, their delight in Nature, not as a pantheistic manifestation, but as a delightful and complicated toy? Is it the absence of all bitterness from their godlike laughter, an absence of bitterness not due, as in the work of our modern

English cartoonists, to a mawkish desire to hurt nobody's feelings, but to an innate loftiness of soul? One cannot say exactly, but I think that many English readers of Paul Fort will admit that had Shakespeare been born a Frenchman of to-day he would have written, at least when in comic or lyric mood, work closely resembling this. One might even add that Shakespeare handles his classical subject in "Venus and Adonis" much as Paul Fort has handled "Les Néréïdes," and, as if to clinch our argument, what insight do the little poems—some of them already quoted—on Hamlet, Ophelia, Lear, show into even the tragic Shakespeare! Few French poets ought to be so profoundly appreciated by English readers.